Acting
from a
Spiritual Perspective

YOUR ART
YOUR BUSINESS
AND YOUR CALLING

Kathryn Marie Bild

CAREER DEVELOPMENT SERIES

A Smith and Kraus Book

Published by
Smith and Kraus, Inc.
177 Lyme Road, Hanover, NH 03755
www.SmithKraus.com

First edition: July 2002
9 8 7 6 5 4 3 2 1

Cover and Text Design by Freedom Hill Design, Reading, Vermont
Cover photo by Doreen Stone
Cover illustration by Lisa Goldfinger

Library of Congress Cataloging-In-Publication Data
Bild, Kathryn Marie.
Acting from a spiritual perspective : your art, your business, and you calling / by Kathryn Marie Bild.
p. cm. — (Career development series)
ISBN 1-57525-294-5
1. Acting—Pyschological aspects. I. Title. II. Series.

PN2058 .B55 2002
792'.028'019—dc21
2002276537

ACKNOWLEDGMENTS

I am grateful to many for their love and support, and for their help in bringing this book to completion. Thank you, first, to Hazel Fitzrandolph who first told me that I was a writer, my brother for telling me I was a director, my cousin Steven Anders who tells me that I am his hero, my mother for supporting my efforts, my sister for her compassion, and my father who not only taught me that I could do anything that a boy could do but whose tender love rescued me from my darkest hour. I miss you, Daddy. And thanks to Angela Hoover, my talented student and friend, for believing in this work and so generously going to bat for me.

Thank you to my eighth grade teacher, Mother Francis Paul, who awakened in me my love for the spoken word, to my spiritual teachers, and to my acting teachers Frank London, Stella Adler, and especially Ed DeLeo and Lorrie Hull who taught me and then for whom I later began to teach. I thank God for giving me the opportunity to then teach on a bigger scale, and the sense to take it—it has led to so many good things, Roxanne Griffin who first gave me the idea to do so, The Bodhi Tree Bookstore and Annex in Los Angeles for allowing me to present for the first time, in lecture form, the ideas that would later develop into this book, and Lora Witty who assisted me at that lecture and first told me that the ideas were good.

I am grateful to my agent Sheree Bykofsky and, especially, my friend and agent Janet Rosen for helping me get the book ready to sell and for keeping the faith that it would. I am grateful for the pleasure of working with a great team of professionals at Smith and Kraus Publishers: Marisa Smith, Eric Kraus; Julia Gignoux from Freedom Hill Design; and Elizabeth Monteleone from Borderlands Press. I can't thank them enough for their commitment, creativity, and kindness. And a humble thanks to those artists and thinkers who have so generously given this book their endorsement.

I thank Valerie Collings and Katherine Braun Mankin, my friends throughout the years who—in addition to being my playmates—have been patient with me when I have been afraid and pointed me to the light when I was down but have never tried to rein me in when I'm flying. A very special thanks to my sweetheart, Conn Horgan who tells me that he loves me and reminds me to keep the faith and be brave, and whose dedication to truth in his life and in his acting is inspiring. And thanks to my departed little buddies Annie, (my golden retriever) and Noah the cat who sat with me in my garden in West Hollywood when I began this book and Magnolia, my new little kitten, who is curled up on my desk with me now in New York as I finish it, for their delightful and comforting company.

Most of all, thanks to my fabulous students, from whom I learn much more than I can ever teach.

for my mother and father

CONTENTS

Part I: What It Is You Are Doing
Inspiration and the Art of Acting

Part II: How to Do It
*Insight on How to Work
More Effectively on Your Craft*

Part III: Overcoming the Obstacles to Doing It
Encouragement and the Business of Acting

Part IV: Why You Do It
Acknowledging Acting As Your Calling

PREFACE

"A great deal of talent is lost to the world for want of a little courage," said Sydney Smith, a clergyman of the nineteenth century who championed the rights of the oppressed. "Every day sends to their graves obscure men and women whom timidity prevented from making a first effort."

How poignantly true that is. How often have we allowed timidity, stage fright—fear in any of its forms—to keep us from even attempting something that we would at least like to try? It sneaks up on us when we are least expecting it and, at the very least, ruins our day.

Not long ago my mother treated our family to a trip to Sea World in San Diego. One of the events we attended was watching three killer whales perform tricks in a huge pool. Before the performance, a trainer selected two members from the audience of over three thousand to stand on a platform that hung over the pool, call out a couple of commands to the whales who would willingly obey them, and then kneel down and rub the tummy of one of the cooperating whales. Two out of three thousand, and I was one of the two. What were the chances of that? One in fifteen hundred, right? And what did I say when the wet-suited performer picked me out of the crowd and extended the invitation? "No way!" I still can't believe it, but I did. "No way!" Then I laughed nervously, stupidly, and the performer asked the woman seated behind me to do it. And the woman happily agreed to.

Realizing what I had just done, I fell immediately into a funk. I—an acting coach and personal success coach who warns people all day long to watch out for just this sort of self-sabotage; someone who, for much of her life, has wrestled with insecurity, inhibition, and stage fright in her own efforts and thought she had finally gotten hold of it—had once again taken the bait and fallen deep into fear's dreary hole. Given the opportunity to interact with and pet a huge killer whale, I had, without even thinking about it, said, "No way!" And why the hell not?! Not because I was afraid of the whale, but because I was afraid, period. The chance of my getting this opportunity in the first place was slim. What is the chance that I will get it ever again? Not too good, right? I blew it. I'd listened to fear, and life and its joys—and its killer whales—had sailed right on past me.

I was mad at myself for a month. Wouldn't even talk to myself! But then I realized, hey, learn from it. You're a schmo, but learn from it. Because, obviously, I still had plenty to learn. Think before you speak, for one thing, I reminded myself, and watch out a little more carefully for the dormant demons of insecurity and timidity just waiting to rob you of your bliss in exchange for a life of safe, unchallenging boredom. It's one of life's greatest tragedies that we let opportunities go by because we're too scared to say, "Thanks, God," and grab them. It hurts to recall them, doesn't it? Just think, we all could have been stars by now—not to mention rich.

It's said by caretaking professionals that the deepest regrets people have on their deathbeds are over the things that they didn't do. "It might have been." That's what gets them—not what they *did* do. And not because they didn't have the opportunities either, but because for one reason or another they failed to take them. "Every day sends to their graves obscure men and women whom timidity prevented from making a first effort," an effort that many men and women, as they lie dying, wish they had made.

Are you going to be one of those people? You don't have

to be. You may blow it occasionally like I did—and do—but you don't, in the long run, have to be one of life's sorrow-filled, remorse-racked losers. No matter how long you have denied or postponed your deepest desires, there's still time. If the bell hasn't rung yet, there's time. The belief that time is running out is just one of the little demons that paralyzes and prevents you from making that first, or next, effort in your field of self-expression. There's a large contingent who believe that, even after the bell has rung, it's still not too late. But whether we go on past the bell or just up to it, we might as well use whatever time we do have doing what we really want to do.

For the purpose of this book, I will assume it is acting. But whether your particular form of creative self-expression is acting or something else, you can be certain that you do have one. At least one. Nobody shows up on this planet who doesn't have some sort of creative bent—whether in the arts or invention or manufacturing or science or healing—because everyone, by nature, is an artist. And life is sweeter and more meaningful to us when we acknowledge our talent and start practicing it.

The focus of this book—as well as the paradigm that elucidates its underlying spiritual principles—is the art of acting: one of the most joyful, enlightening, confidence-building, and metaphysical of the arts. And although this book embraces Stanislavski's System and Strasberg's Method as its basis for practical, hands-on technique, the emphasis is on the nature and value of acting from the spiritual point of view—its essence; its integration as an art, a business, and a calling; and its role in the evolution of the soul, not only of the actor, but of the society, which benefits from the actor's contribution. The principles themselves are not limited to acting, however; they may be applied to any creative or positive venture.

I first became interested in the arts when I was a small child. My mother says I sang in my crib. I have been singing ever since and I love it, although for many years I was afflicted with such intense insecurity and inhibition that I sang only when I was alone. So I know how it feels to be blocked. I'll give you a short history of my first stab at the arts so you'll know what I mean.

I began writing poetry when I was ten, songs and stories soon after that, and the first of many sketches for plays and novels and nonfiction books after that. But my confidence in my writer's voice as I grew seemed to diminish in proportion to my expanding awareness of the world around me. By the time I was fifteen, everything I wanted to say seemed either already said or shallow, which, in spite of the fact that the urge to express myself was intensifying to the point of desperation, blocked my ability to express anything at all.

I also tried dancing for a while. I had begun taking ballet lessons when I was three as a corrective because I was badly bow-legged. I took lessons on and off (mostly off) until I was twelve and considered myself something of a ballerina, until one Saturday afternoon when I attended a recital starring my friend Lilly who I thought was on the same level I was and I was jolted by the vision of what a burgeoning ballerina really looked like. As a result, ballet fell with a thud in my life from a potential career to a mere form of exercise.

As a teen I tried the visual arts. I tried drawing but had neither the confidence nor the patience for it; tried painting, which was fun but messy; did a little clay sculpting, which was forgettable; and threw a few pots—which never were heard from again.

Meanwhile, I had started acting and directing in my own little theater in our backyard by the time I was nine. There, as with singing, I had found my bliss but I didn't know it. I wrote the plays, cast them, starred in them, directed them, advertised them, made and sold tickets from my homemade cardboard-box-on-a-tray-table box office for them, and during intermission sold the popcorn and lemonade I'd made. This theatrical heyday lasted for only a couple of years, however; even before my writer's voice took a dive at fifteen, I had become too "sophisticated" and self-conscious for homegrown, grassroots theater. So by the time I was twelve, I had closed down my theater.

Finally, not long before my sixteenth birthday, I woke up one morning with the horrible realization that I had become thoroughly blocked and mute. It was as if, during the preceding five years, my entire being had been pounded, pushed down, and shoved into a tiny two-inch pill box while, at the same time, I was pulsing with an increasingly urgent creative energy so explosive that I felt that if I could unleash it, my squished little, two-inch being would burst forth to the size of Godzilla. I wanted to sing! But I was scared. I wanted to write! But I felt stupid. I wanted to dance! But I was a klutz. I wanted to draw and paint and sculpt! But I was scattered, insecure, and unfocused. I wanted to act in and direct more theater! But I was held captive in some tiny, forbidding never-never land between quasi-intelligence and innocence. I felt desperate but paralyzed, like a motor turned on high but whose parts were all frozen; my nerves were exhausted and frazzled by the constantly thwarted effort. And yet, I wanted to do it *all*, which was another problem. I was too desperately hungry to do *everything*, to calm down enough to choose *anything*, and then start on the road to doing *something* long enough to get good at it. I was an average girl with average talent, above average ambition, too little focus, very little discipline, and almost no guidance. Nor had I any inkling at the time that the neuro-nuclear pressure in my consciousness was forming precious creative jewels that would eventually crystallize, ready for mining, like the black opals, sapphires, and diamonds formed by the excessive heat from underground nuclear test blasts conducted in the desert by NASA. I only knew that I was miserable.

And yet, my desires would prove stronger than the obstacles that forged them. My path seemed to become increasingly creatively circuitous and lead me away from art altogether for a long while—to teenage modeling and commercial acting, not stage or film acting; to a five-year stint producing television commercials, not directing theater or film; to working on the business side of the business, not the creative, artistic side; even to partnering with and marrying an actor/singer/songwriter but not *being* an actor/singer/songwriter. But I was learning and paying dues—dues exacted only by myself, it turns out; for some reason I believed I needed to earn as an adult the right to do what had come so naturally to me as a child.

It was slow going at first and it took years. And once I had made it past myself, I then had to fight, tooth and nail, the gatekeepers I had enlisted as partners in my oppression, the ones who had answered my declaration that I was neither capable nor worthy to be an artist by only too eagerly enlisting me to serve them in their being artists. But I persevered. And in the end, their resistance proved to have been only more concrete through which to bust, more pressure out of which would eventually pop the precious jewels of my future artistic expression. Even before I freed myself of a bad marriage and was able to correct another difficult relationship, I began to write again. I wrote and directed two short films, produced a full-length video for which I received the Grammy's Video Producer of the Year Award, and I submitted one of my screenplays to the American Film Institute's Directing Workshop for Women and was selected to go through the program, during which I produced and directed an hour-long version of my screenplay. But by this time I was in my late thirties and I was worrying it was already too late to "make it," especially since I still wasn't ready to focus in any one area. I had some catching up and experimenting to do first.

The first thing I did as a free bird was to sing. I had been taking voice lessons on and off as a hobby, but now I went at it full tilt. Before my divorce, I wouldn't sing in front of anyone. Now, no one could get me to shut up. I grabbed everyone who came over, from friends, nephews, and stepkids to the telephone installation guy, and made them sit down and listen to me sing twenty-five songs in succession.

Next, I started working on two books that I'd been wanting to write. I established goals, set deadlines, and met them—after extending them a few times. It was much harder than I thought it would be. I found that I needed to learn how to do it, which went far beyond just my desire and willingness to do it. But I was learning; I was making it through the trenches.

Finally, I took up the study of acting. For years I had been craving to understand acting as an art and a craft, but I was too afraid to take a class. Now, having burst from my box of terror, I couldn't wait to get at it. Not that I was no longer afraid: I was. But I was no longer allowing my fears to rule me. I started reading everything on acting that I could get my hands on—Stanislavski, Strasberg, Hagan, Adler, Hull, Meisner, Lewis—and for the next three years I studied intensively with Stella Adler, Lorrie Hull, Frank London, Ed DeLeo, and others.

The more I read and trained and performed, the more I was intrigued by the beautiful mystique of acting. Acting, which I had so loved as a child, now spoke to me as one of the more compassionate and consciousness-raising of the arts. And it was through the art of acting, more than any other, that I discovered that one learns, grows, becomes, is, and then gives as an artist. I further discovered that, while acting would not become my main area of artistic *practice*, it was and would remain—as it had been since I was nine years old—pivotal in my life as the artist and teacher that I was becoming. For although the heart of the drama is the story, the soul of the story is the acting—that which is going on with and between the people in the story on the page, the stage, or the screen. It runs the gamut of human experience. It is metaphysical in that it deals deeply in the realm of pure consciousness, while, at the same time, it is the rawest and most human of the arts because actors, when acting, are simply acting the way people act. No sugar, no bullshit, no kidding. I saw that this undressed truth in thought, feeling, and action, which dramatic acting contributes to society, is crucial to the success and well-being not only of all art, but of every human life. I was finally finding my way.

In addition to artistic challenges, which included such questions as "What shall I be?" and "Do I have the right, the nerve and the ability to be it?," my journey has also been driven by even deeper soul-searching questions: If I do succeed in figuring out what I want to be, how do I reconcile what I *want* to do with what I think I *should* do? Should I choose business or art? Which is higher? If art is higher, is it high enough? Is it self-indulgent? Should I choose service (ministry, counseling, teaching)? If I choose business or art, though, how do I blend my career with my mission or life purpose to make my life worthwhile? Is it *possible* for my self-expression, my career, and my mission (my art, my business, and my calling) to be one?

Throughout my life, my endeavors and my quest for the answers to these questions have combined to be the impetus and objective of my own life journey. Today, nearly fifteen years after my artistic wings once again began to take flight, I am writing novels, screenplays, books like this one, and songs; I'm directing film; I privately coach actors and directors and do a little acting and singing myself; and I coach people in other occupations for personal success—all of which I adore. I'm on my path. What's more, as circuitous as it has seemed, I now see that I always have been on my path. And yet, I believe it would have been more direct, faster, and less painful if I had had the benefit of good coaching.

That is the reason I started teaching, and it is the reason I have written this book. I am hopeful that this book will help you to get on track a bit faster than I did. I understand how hard it is to determine and then go after what you want. I know the face of the enemy that sets mental and emotional, not to mention physical and economic, obstacles before our every footstep. I understand, and you have my compassion. What's more, you have my love and support. Hopefully, within these pages, I can offer you some of the wisdom and guidance I wish I'd had when I was setting out on my own journey. I believe that a clear understanding of what it really is that you're going after, as well as a few helpful suggestions about how to navigate the pitfalls you will encounter along the way, demystifies the goal and makes it more easily achievable. Oh, you'll get there either way, just as I have gotten here. Life is foolproof, and it truly is never too late. I believe that. But if that's true, then it's never too early, either. Success is a God-given gift to which every last one of us is entitled. Let us accept that gift with humility—what a teacher of mine defined as "the understanding of one's place in the world as the effect, and recipient, of all that is truly magnificent."

Acting from the spiritual perspective, then, is the perception of what acting is in its essence, which is entitled to reverence and respect. When you see acting this way, see it for what it really is, not as a luxury but as a necessary facility of society, you begin to realize that when it is done correctly, the practice of acting is as powerful in its function as church.

I'd like to ask you to make an agreement with me before we begin. While you read this book, let's all be actors together. We'll all be members of Actors Anonymous, say. That way, you will be getting what I'm saying directly, from the inside. You're an actor—OK? So from the insider's point of view, you are about to take a good look at acting from the spiritual—and most practical—perspective.

Part I

WHAT IT IS
YOU ARE DOING

*Inspiration
and the
Art of Acting*

CHAPTER 1

Our Spiritual Workshop

Man is asked to make of himself what he is supposed
to become to fulfill his destiny.

—Paul Tillich

We are on a pilgrimage during our course of life here on Earth. The destination of our pilgrimage is our own self-fulfillment, which we achieve through a series of spiritual assignments or workshops, as I prefer to call them, through which we learn our major lessons and grow to our next stage of development. Our career is one of the workshops. It is not our only workshop; relationships, for instance, are workshops, too. But certainly every career or occupation is one of the major workshops in our lives by which we learn to express such qualities as patience, creativity, and courage.

THE PURPOSE OF OUR PILGRIMAGE

Although there is some choice of specifics within the workshops, we are all on essentially the same pilgrimage, and the pilgrimage itself has a fixed purpose. Put another way, this "Earth school" or *university* where we take this pilgrimage offers only one major. We are here to major in discovering and demonstrating our divinity—our dominion—which, as radical as it may at first sound, means developing our mastery over all forms of "evil."

THE CURRICULUM OF WORKSHOPS

Just as a university major has within its curriculum some choice as to the specific classes that meet its requirements, so it is in our experience here on Earth. In a university's fine arts major, for instance, you may be required to take an art class, but you are given the choice between classes in painting, drawing, or sculpting. And you may have to take a foreign language class, but it's up to you to choose Japanese, Spanish, or Russian. So it is in the "big" school. Within our life major, the three main assigned workshops by which we achieve the purpose of our pilgrimage are our careers, our relationships, and our mental and physical health. Together, these workshops combine to constitute our one common major in the overall curriculum on Earth. And although there is room for some choices within them, everybody has to take these three workshops. For the purposes of this book, I am focusing on the workshop of our career and the specific career choice of acting.

We all have careers, whether we call it that or not, because we all work. And we have some selection as to the type of career we practice—but not much, when you think about it. There are only a handful of main categories. We've got art, science, business, health services, education, and the clergy. Within each of these, there is a variety of specific choices, yes; but there aren't really that many of those, either. Of course, you may be a maverick and forge your own, but this will probably prove to be an offshoot or synthesis of others. This limitation is not a bad thing, however. On the contrary, the fact that our choices are

3

confined is a blessing. It's not the career itself that is most important but the growth we achieve through its practice. And the fewer the options, the sooner we are able to sift through them, choose one, and commit to learning its lessons.

I find it fascinating that almost any career choice you make—within certain limits, of course—will help you make the discoveries and demonstrations divinely assigned to you. In choosing or developing one, then, you want to be sure that you pick one that challenges you, that has within it nothing that opposes or is inconsistent with your spiritual growth, and that you *like*. With this three-part proviso met, it doesn't really matter which career you choose since every human occupation is a spiritual workshop. The same spiritual principles and concepts apply equally to each, and you get the same benefits of understanding and growth from all of them. What the choice comes down to, then, is your own individual call, your instinct, your intuition, your *desire*. Can you honestly say to yourself, "This work can and shall be my means of expressing myself, my means of exchange, and my way of serving the world—in other words, my art, my business, and my calling—because I would *like* it to be?" If you can, then, it will do. You can see how crucial it is, though, for you to pick something you want to do, something that you can stay with, grow from, get better at, and continue to love more and more as you explore and walk in its path.

❀ *Affirmation*
I love to be doing only that which is truly good for me.

ACTING AS A CAREER CHOICE

I think that acting is one of the best career choices offered to us. Whether on stage or in front of the camera, it is a tremendously effective means by which to learn and grow; it is well balanced as an art, a business, and a calling; and last, but not least, it's a blast!

We live in a world where we have to make a living. And the fact that we do provides us with a certain structure that can help us if we let it, in the same way that structural parameters can be helpful to a fine artist. If you're instructed to paint a painting on a wooden plank of a certain size and to use black and green but no red, rather than limiting you, these parameters can become a blast-off point for creative imagination. So it can be with making a living. Like it or not, we have to do it, so we might as well pick a career that is consistent with the objectives of our pilgrimage and that gives us a few laughs in the process. People have various ideas about what heaven is. We can all agree, however, that heaven on Earth includes making a living doing something we love to do. If it's your way, acting is a great way to do that. But whatever you choose as your way, it will only truly *be* your way if you love it.

✖ EXERCISE

Be seven years old again and answer the question, What do you want to be when you grow up?

_____

_____

ACTING AS AN OCCUPATION

Like all right livelihood, acting provides the actor many valuable opportunities to develop and express his or her abilities. It requires great intelligence to be a good actor and great compassion. You have to really understand the human condition, the intricacies of consciousness, and the psychological elements that play upon or come up against one another within relationships. You have to understand the deepest human desires and motives, as well as the neuroses, fears, and inhibitions that resist and retard the expression of those desires and motives. By trafficking in this human mental makeup on a daily basis as your work, you, the actor, gain the understanding that eventually makes you a great actor. You realize, "This is how people behave, interact, and *are*. This is how *I* am. This is the way that *it is*." It requires lots of courage to be a performer, to get up there and lift up your shirt and say, "Here I am. This is what I've got," and to not only trust that it is enough, but that it is worthy of honor and respect. It is by dealing in these elements on a daily basis, in your spiritual career workshop called acting, that you develop your spiritual musculature.

Your living commitment to this work is one of the great ways by which you bless yourself. And doing it well gives you the opportunity, as well as the forum, to bless others. The folks with the power to hire you see that, yes, you get the gist of how this acting stuff works and they hire you. The audience comes in, they give you their admission fee, a certain amount of trust that you're going to give them something back, and they sit in the dark, captive, while you perform the palpable service of elucidating truth for them and, at the same time, entertain the socks off them. Then they, delighted, refreshed, and *bettered*, go out and use that truth to bless others besides themselves, and everyone is richer for the experience. Not a bad day's work on the part of the actor.

Another good thing about being an actor is that it doesn't matter who you are or what you look like. If you're a person, then you are already qualified to represent a substantial contingent of humanity. When you are ready to demonstrate that you know how to do that on stage, you're ready to be an actor. Other people—agents, casting directors, directors, producers— will also be able to see that you can do it and do it well, and you will have become "supply" to their and society's "demand." Opportunities will arise accordingly, which will lead to your satisfying and dependable prosperity.

PROSPERITY: A BY-PRODUCT OF PERSISTENCE

Prosperity is one heck of an interesting subject to us, isn't it? More than that, it is one of the most sought after conditions of reality. The good news is that it *is* a condition of reality, an unalterable condition. Life prospers. It's one of the things that life does. Therefore, as little "life-ettes," so do we. We are continually provided with the inspiration and opportunities to grow and prosper by using those opportunities to not only pay our bills but—because we've been able to—to focus on our work, which will lead us to produce even better and richer work, which will enable us to prosper more. All this comes as a result of your choosing the right spiritual workshop—the one you *wanted*—and committing to doing the work fully.

THE FULLY STOCKED SCHOOLHOUSE—OUR EARTH

This place of our pilgrimage, our Earth, is a manifestation of the concept of *place* and *residence*. It resides first within our own consciousness and then manifests as our fully stocked, self-sufficient planet. All that we need—every thing and every idea—for the successful completion of our pilgrimage assignments to learn and grow is provided and is at our disposal, *here and now*. Not only is it provided, but we always have free access to it. It is ours. We have water. We have food. We have a place to lie down and refresh ourselves when we're tired. We have inspiration and guidance. We have humor to get us over the rough spots and faith when we lose the light. All of it is ours, everything we need to succeed in our overall mission of demonstrating our dominion and overcoming limitations and all fear that anything has power over us. And all of it belongs to each and every one of us. Every last one of us is rich!

SUPPORTIVE RELATIONSHIPS

In addition to what we need for our physical well-being (water, food, shelter, clothing) and what we need for our mental well-being (faith, guidance, inspiration), *we have the emotional support of loving and nurturing relationships.*

✳ EXERCISE

> **Take a moment and check one of the following. That last statement was: ____ True ____ False**

If you checked false, then you have some immediate work to do, because relationships that do not support you have got to go. You've got to transform or dump them. You cannot hold on to unsupportive relationships. Mothers are supposed to mother you. Fathers are supposed to father you. Friends are supposed to befriend you. And lovers are supposed to love you. You get the idea? Their *purpose* in your life, the underlying purpose of all of them, is to *support* you in your life and your work. If they don't, or don't any longer, then it's outski! You do not need them—on the contrary. If people neglect, belittle, accuse, or abuse you, and you've spoken to them about this and they keep doing it, say good night, Gracie.

It is my belief that our work comes first in our lives. Not merely our careers, but our life's work, and not to the exclusion of our relationships. But I do believe that your pilgrimage on the planet comes first. You come here alone to achieve certain results and you leave alone, hopefully having achieved them. Any relationships you form once you get here are therefore, by nature, secondary—not to mention temporary—and they have got to support your mission, or they have no worthy function in your life. If they are detrimental, they must be terminated. We have joy, humor, direction, and guidance, and we have the energy to act. We have all that we need to successfully achieve our mission, and all of it is already within ourselves. We don't need anyone else for any of that. We need one another for support, comfort, and fun. So find people that give you those things, and don't waste any of your precious time with energy-sucking noodle brains who don't. Please!

❋ EXERCISE

Complete the following sentence: If I treated my own desires more seriously and did what I truly wanted,

_____

_____

WHAT IS REQUIRED OF US?

We've talked about what we need from careers that are worthy and relationships that are worthwhile, but what about what is required of each of us on this pilgrimage? What is required of us in terms of attitude and intention on this assignment? In a word, what is required of us is *commitment*, which I believe consists of four main components:

1. First of all, we must accept our mission to grow. Accept it. Embrace it. Love it. I always feel sorry for people who say they didn't like, or don't like, school. I think that is such a tragedy. It's a shame that no one ever explained to them that more than giving us information, the learning process teaches us to think effectively and critically so that when we gather information more useful to us than the topics we learned in school—information about life itself—we will know how to embrace it. The joy of learning, the joy of those moments when the light goes on and we fully understand something—how spectacular that is! The satisfaction of companioning with the masters through their writings, as well as with those on the learning

path with us, is a wonderful thing. It is natural for us to continue to learn and to grow all our lives. And accepting our mission to grow is the number one requirement of committing to our pilgrimage.

2. We must trust that our mission will succeed. We are choosing acting as our career for many reasons—universal and personal, deep and light. These reasons will clarify and evolve as we proceed, but the point is that they are valid and, ultimately, we *will* succeed. We will become good actors and we will grow. This victory will not necessarily come easily, however. We will battle outer resistance that says we can't do it, and then, once that battle is won, we will battle inner resistance, our own self-doubt . By using trust as a weapon, we will fight. We will say, "I will be an actor because I want to be one. I accept my mission to be an actor, a mission that, by my own desire, I give to myself." And that is the way it should be, because we are blessed with the gift of unthwartable dominion. And you may, and *must*, trust that the choices of your will shall succeed.

Yes, you have all that you need to succeed. Therefore, there is no legitimate cause for worry or fear. Not to say that fear won't still haunt you for a time, unfortunately. As St. Paul put it, "the weapons of our warfare are not carnal," and neither are the enemies we fight with those weapons. But such enemies as fear, doubt, and resistance—the mental obstacles we come up against and by which we grow in our spiritual workshops— are incapable of defeating us in the ultimate success of our missions.

3. In addition to accepting our mission to grow and trusting that we will succeed in it, the third thing that is required of us is dedicated effort in our specific career workshop. Dedication. No sloth. Do it every day. Act every day. Every day you are an actor. That is your work—every day. You have become clear that your work is to grow, to honor life, and to bless society through acting. From now on, then, spend a portion of every day acting. Whether that means you read plays, talk to

other actors about plays, learn another monologue, or read a book on playwriting or directing, do something involving your craft every day. Our success in the career of acting, as in any career, is of less importance to us in the long run than our dedication and effort toward it, for it *is* how you play the game that counts. Not to say that it isn't a game that you want to win, but you're more likely to win the game, as well as become more worthy of winning, in proportion to your dedicated efforts toward it. So work at it.

4. The fourth component of the commitment that is required of us on our pilgrimage toward greater understanding of ourselves is brotherly kindness and compassion for our fellow pilgrims. Love.

✷ EXERCISE

Using a tape recorder, please sing about something that you're happy about. Just turn on the recorder and sing. Make it musical, but don't try to make it rhyme. When you feel you have fully expressed yourself, you have finished.

THE SUCCESSFUL ACTOR

It is not within our power to succeed. I know that is a tough statement and, on the surface, flies in the face of what I have just said. But it is true. You can do your best, but you can't make people like your work. You can't make people hire you. You can't make people buy your product.

The good news is that you and I are part of a fabulous, successful system. And if you do your part in the system, you can trust that the system, or life, will do its part—which is a very good thing because if the system itself didn't work, we'd all be in a lot of trouble! Others buy my product, and will continue to buy my product, because my product, by nature, is desirable, and I succeed because life is successful. I can depend on that, and that's great.

But there is something to watch out for here. To the degree that my desire for business success supersedes my objective to grow and self-actualize, my efforts become a spiritual detour. I lose my focus, my efficacy as a businesswoman, and my comfort. So what are we to do? For we do want to succeed. There is only one thing for us to do. We go for the gold. We learn as much as we can about life, become the best actors that we can be, put into practice what we learn, and trust—in fact, insist—that our work and our lives will succeed. We count on the promise that if we work with commitment, all our needs will be met. And met how? In some paltry, subsistence-level way? No. If God is love, and God is, then our needs will be met abundantly.

LIFE, THE ONLY EMPLOYER

After all, it would be stupid for life to do less than abundantly meet our needs, wouldn't it? Because if life, or God, wants us to self-actualize as perfect manifestations of itself, by which the whole is honored, it's in life's own self-interest to assure our prosperity—assuming that God is at least as intelligent as we are!—so that we will continue to contribute to the ongoing functioning of the one perfect system. So don't worry; your success is assured!

EXERCISE

Assume that you are completely successful. You have achieved all that you wish to achieve. Now, dictate a letter to God that, afterward, you (or one of your secretaries) will type up and send. (Where, I'm not sure. Heaven, I s'pose.) Do not censor yourself. Say whatever comes into your mind.

You can edit later. When you feel you have fully expressed yourself, you have finished.

Remember, we're here only a few years, and then we're moving on to the next stop-off point, so getting the big cars and the houses is all very well and good and fun, but it's also very temporary. And we all know that. So, let's get real here. We do have to eat, but let's keep our eyes on the doughnut and not on the hole. If our eyes are on the hole, which we then keep trying to fill with "stuff," we are not going to achieve the greater wealth of satisfaction, which will remain with us forever.

THE DIAMOND OF DESIRE

Desire is your friend. Desire is a psychic diamond. It glistens and points you in the right direction. Follow it. You can trust it. It is incorrect to think that your desires will lead you wrong or that human will is against God's will. There is only one mind; therefore, there is only one will. And it is the same mind and will that is possessed by each of us. You can trust, therefore, that your desires will lead you in the right way.

We used to think, incorrectly, that our impulses were evil and would lead us down the garden path, so it would be better for us to do what we *didn't* want to do. But life is not a trick. Nobody's trying to lead you in the wrong direction, which you've then got to try to straighten out by some cruel, cryptic code of opposites. It's simple. Do what you want to do. That's how you know what you "should" do.

"But, I want to succeed," you say. "in *this* world. *Now!*" Of course you do. Who doesn't? At its deepest level that impulse is divine. The wanting and trying to succeed by creating a product or service worthy of selling—in our case, acting—inevitably fuels our progress.

13

SUCCESS IS INEVITABLE

More than succeeding within a career workshop, though, I value knowing that I am succeeding in the purpose of my pilgrimage, in understanding and demonstrating the magnificence that I, as an expression of life, am. That's what matters most. Furthermore, I know I can count on my life being fully "funded," which means that I will have all the opportunities I need, no matter how many it takes, as well as everything else necessary for me to grow and succeed according to life's design. Because, eventually, everyone makes it—even the schmos—for life is good and it is our magnificent mission to live the fact that it is.

✷ EXERCISE

Cup your hands and imagine you are holding a portion of the cosmos. Now allow the Earth to appear in the middle of your hands. Hold her, support her, buoy her. Look on her as though she and all her inhabitants are solely in your care. Watch her turn on her axis. Then, continent by continent, zoom in on a household on each of the seven continents. See the exterior, then the interior of the house. See the people and animals that inhabit the house. Use your imagination and see the details. Listen to the goings-on in that house. Understand, forgive if necessary, and love each person in that house, then zoom back out and go to the next continent. When you have completed the seven visits, again see the planet as a sphere in your hands. See its color and textures and movement. When you feel you have thoroughly observed and loved her as her only caretaker, you have finished. You may then bless her and place her back safely in the heavens.

SUMMARY OF MAIN POINTS

1. Our career is one of the workshops we take during our pilgrimage on Earth by which we grow in discovering and developing our full potential.

2. Our career, our relationships, and our health are the three main workshops, or constituents, of our common Earth major. Each workshop has a variety of choices. This book focuses on the career choice of acting.

3. In choosing a career, it is important to pick one that challenges you; that has nothing within it that opposes your spiritual growth; that stands well balanced on the three legs of being your art, your business, and your calling; and that you like.

4. Acting, if it is your way, is a great career that meets all these standards. By trafficking in the human mental makeup on a daily basis, the actor gains compassion and insight, which not only makes him or her a great actor, but also helps to develop him or her as an individual.

5. All that we need for our pilgrimage, as well as for the success of our career, is provided and is at our disposal—including our knowledge of this fact.

6. Your mission on Earth comes first. The main purpose of relationships in your life is to support you and your work. Those that do not have got to go.

7. During our pilgrimage four components of commitment are required of us:
   - Acceptance of our mission to grow
   - Trust that our mission will succeed
   - Dedicated effort in our specific career workshop in which that growth occurs
   - Brotherly kindness and compassion for our fellow pilgrims

8. It is not within your personal power to succeed. But, fortunately, you are part of a system—life or God—and God

15

is the prospering principle. You succeed, therefore, because the system is successful.

9. It is in life's self-interest to make sure that you succeed and are abundantly compensated for doing so, so that you will continue to contribute to the ever-continuing functioning of life.

10. Desire is your friend. It is the psychic diamond that points the way for you. What you want to do is what you should do, and you will become truly successful only once you are doing that.

CHAPTER 2

The Quest for Permission

> *When you talk in terms of artistic creation, the permission . . . comes not from the society but from within oneself.*
>
> —Jeanne Moreau

When I was a little girl, struck dumb by stage fright after having been asked to sing for my relatives during a family gathering, I believed that my salvation would come if everyone would just applaud and praise me before I even opened my mouth. If I could have the applause beforehand, or at least be 100 percent sure that I'd get it afterward, then I would be able to proceed without fear, I thought; and it seemed perfectly reasonable to me that it should happen that way, too. However, it never did.

THE KEY TO FINDING APPROVAL

Apparently, I'm not alone. I can't tell you how many of my students and clients have told me that they crave approval and acceptance. We all do. We all want to be valued and loved and appreciated. That is a normal human desire. When Jesus of Nazareth was baptized in the River Jordan by John the Baptist, what were the first words he heard following the ceremony? "This is my beloved son in whom I am well pleased." Don't you think that approbation was an outcome of his desire to please and be accepted? Of course it was.

We all have the desire to be pleasing and accepted, and that's not going to go away. But there's a key here. It's a two-part key. First, to get that approbation and acceptance, our objective must be not to please our brothers and sisters, but to please our common source, or God. Second, rather than trying to get it from others, we must recognize that it is already God-given and that through our own acceptance we access it. The relationship with our brothers and sisters, then, is one of companionship because we're all traveling together—a little wink, a little elbow jab in the side: "Hi, I'm on the same path you are." "Yeah, hi, how's it going?" But we don't get our permission to do our work or our approval for having done it from another human being, even though that approval will be reflected in success, which will include our brothers and sisters liking what we do. Your main objective in being an actor then—the primordial one—must be to please your source.

✵ EXERCISE

In every film, play, video, or television show that you watch this week, look for your role. If it's a World War II film and there's only one old woman who takes out the trash—and you're a woman—that's your role. If the show has several parts for your gender, pick the one that is yours. Keep a list of the roles you are playing this week. Notice that many possibilities exist for you.

THE PENALTY FOR THE MISDIRECTED PLEA

What happens, though, if you do try to get your permission from somebody else? We've all been there when we've felt insecure. Sometimes it goes better than others. It certainly isn't dependable, though, depending on another. Nor does it adequately satisfy us even when it goes well, even if the person we're asking says, "Oh, yeah, go for it! You can do it! You're great!" That never gives us the depth of satisfaction or confidence we feel when we get our permission and approval from ourselves. Even worse, if you look to someone else to prop up your sense of self, you will find yourself thinking horribly uncomfortable things like, "Oh, my God, I have to be nice to this person even though he's a dorkhead to me at other times so he'll continue to give me his approval because it could be withdrawn at any moment!" Which, if he gets mad at you, it sure might be.

❀ *Affirmation*

I have real genius within me.

THE DASTARDLY DORKHEADS

You may know that because you are a perfect spiritual being you have real genius within you, but others may not. Others may suspect it but envy you because they don't think much of themselves, and so they purposefully withhold the permission to act that you are mistakenly seeking from outside yourself. Is that really true? You betcha. And who are they? Oh, only the people supposedly closest to you, your family and friends and lovers. Your father who will say "Get a real job." Your mother who will say "tsk" and laugh.

Generally, the people who withhold their permission—not that it's theirs to give—are those who are angry with themselves because they didn't follow their own dreams and desires. And there are quite a few of them. So you're in treacherous territory if you're trying to get your permission from other people. That's not the biggest problem with it, though. The biggest problem is that you wander off your spiritual base when you set up a false, idolatrous authority—which, by its very nature, is destined to fall. Rather than getting off on that sidetrack, make up your own mind. Let the winds blow and the fear swirl around you, and let people say you're being stupid or shallow or selfish to follow your dream to be an actor. And then go right ahead and do it.

I AM AN ACTOR!

Now, what do you say when somebody asks you if you are an actor? This is a big scary moment, right?

"Uh, yes, I am," you might say.

"Really? What have you done?"

"Oh, nothing. Um. But I'm trying."

"Oh, so you're *trying* to be an actor."

"Well, no, I'm more than just trying . . . ," you might manage to get out.

"Oh, oh. I see. OK. Right," your interrogator then concludes and walks away with a self-satisfied smile on his face, glad to see that even though you're trying, you're not really doing it, so it makes him feel better that he's not even trying. And it gives him further fodder for his self-justification that it's no use to try either because the chances are so small—I mean, look at *you*. And that will please him because he won't realize that, in fact, he's a duped proponent of the scarcity principle—as if there ever could be such a principle—instead of the principle of abundance and believes that his good is miles away from him and inaccessible. But the interchange won't have been much fun for you.

I suggest when somebody asks you if you're an actor, that you employ one of two answers. You either say yes like above, but with more conviction and confidence. Then, when subjected to further probing—which, inevitably, you will be—answer the questions as honestly and courageously as any other martyr whose ranks you, by the time your interrogator gets done with you, will have joined.

"Really? What have you done?"

"What I have done is I've gotten a book by Stella Adler, a book by Constantine Stanislavski, and a book by Robert Lewis, and I've read the first three chapters of the first two and half of the third and I've enrolled in an acting class."

"Oh, so you're studying to be an actor?"

"Yes, I am."

"Oh, but you said you were an actor."

"Yes, I did." And you can leave it there or you can explain, "Because that's what an actor does. I'm at the beginning of it, but I'm doing it." I mean, is a sapling less a tree because it isn't yet fully grown? No.

Or, if you want to avoid all that scrutiny and waste of your valuable time, you might simply say, "I'm studying to be an actor." That's humble and it deflects attack from the egos of others who hate themselves for their own lack of courage. But the first answer is more accurate. The main point here, however, is that you neither get your permission nor your approbation from outside yourself, so get used to that liberating fact right now!

✳ EXERCISE

Ask someone close to you, whom you suspect might be tempted to criticize you, to listen to you sing a song. Sing the song. While you are singing it, be aware of what your little mental demons are saying inside your head. "This is dumb. I can't do this. She thinks I'm a fruitcake." When you have finished, thank your observer, but neither solicit nor accept any comments on your performance from her. Tell her that your refusal to hear any comments or judgments from her is part of the exercise. Walk away. Now, privately, jot down how this has made you feel.

THE HELPFUL LETDOWN

When you give your power away to other people, they mirror your underlying insecurity and assumption that you are power-less by withholding their permission from you. "No," you will hear, in words or between the lines, as you yourself have pre-determined, "you *don't* have what it takes. You *can't* do it." It's a painful phenomenon that, sometimes when you are the most down, you get the least help from your friends, lovers, or family. Often, they've just had enough; they don't want to hear it anymore. The greater truth is they're not equipped to give you what only you can provide for yourself.

But that's good. That's helpful to you. Because if they were, that might only make you more dependent on them. So, though it may make you angry, what may appear to you as heartless-ness at a time when you need them the most can have the healthy effect of vitalizing your own self-survival skills. And be honest. When things are reversed, don't you feel the same way toward someone else who comes at you time and again with his or her neediness? We're there for one another to a degree, and for a time, but ultimately each one of us has to get up and go get it ourselves. That's the way the universe is set up, and the way that it should be. So get out of the habit of asking anyone for anything. Become self-reliant. The truth of the matter is nobody else has anything that you truly need.

THE IMPORTANCE OF PROPER IDENTIFICATION

How exactly do we do that, though? How do we become self-reliant? The answer lies in properly identifying ourselves every day.

We are barraged with false labeling. "I am a poorly educated forty-year-old Native American man with little income and no opportunities." "I am a woman and therefore will never get past the glass ceiling." "My father is the head of a film studio, so I have great opportunity to work as an actress but little confidence because my mother gave up her career to marry my father and resents my succeeding in a dream that she forfeited."

Absolute poppycock! And yet, we are barraged with just this sort of false identification. It says that we are separate from our creator, inheritors of our parents' genealogy, victims of our environment, and limited by our education. It says that we had a beginning and will come to an end and that in between we are subject to grave adversity and failure so that there is no use in even trying. That's the picture. Bleak. The Irish have a saying that encapsulates it: "It's a tale of woe from the cradle to the grave." And if I believed that was true, I would put down my pen at this moment and think, "What's the frigging use?"

But you and I—all of us—know, because this God-given jewel of knowledge resides within every human heart, that this bleak and hopeless outlook is false. We know, in fact, that this very point of view is the enemy. It exists solely so we can combat it and, by doing so, demonstrate our strength and dominion. So this "enemy" is not so bad after all. Its suggestions are very frightening to us, yes. But when we courageously accept our assignment to meet and defeat it, we see it is really our ally, a part of our universal support system—which disproves the "tale of woe."

❊ EXERCISE

Into your tape recorder, improvise a three-minute stream of consciousness monologue about a peak experience in your past when you, the star of the experience, exercised power and dominion, which culminated in your saving the day.

Proper identification begins, then, with ceasing to identify ourselves falsely, and then consciously aligning our sense of who we are with our source. We are all perfect spiritual beings, shining stars, the ideal in living forms. We are royalty, the sons and daughters of life and love. That is who you are, and it is by this proper self-identification that you validate your status for yourself and boldly accept your God-given permission to work in your chosen field. It is important to do this for yourself every day. So, onward!

SUMMARY OF MAIN POINTS

1. The approval we all seek comes from pleasing our source.
2. Our permission to follow our heart's desires is God-given, evidenced by the very existence of the desires themselves, and we access that permission by accepting it.
3. Our relationships with our planetary brothers and sisters should be mutually supportive, but you get neither your permission to act nor your approval from other people. You are self-sufficient; no one else has anything that you need.
4. Trying to get what you want or need from some other person is idolatrous and, inevitably, sets you up for a fall. Become self-reliant now.
5. Imperative to your achieving the strong and healthy self-reliance you need to succeed in your life and your career is instituting a daily spiritual practice that will equip you to reject the barrage of false labeling that besieges us every day.
6. This spiritual work begins with proper self-identification.

CHAPTER 3

Into the Vestibule of Preparation

Prepare. Apart from anything else, preparation uses up a lot of the nervous energy that otherwise might rise up to betray you. Channel that energy; focus it into areas that you control.

—Michael Caine

In cold climates, houses have entry rooms or vestibules that keep out the cold air, a room where people take off their boots and coats before entering the main house. The vestibule is a passage point, a protective preparatory way to pass from the outside to the inside. The vestibule of a church is similar; you go through a point of preparation before entering the church.

I think of the relaxation and warm-up exercises that an actor does before acting as a vestibule through which he or she leaves his or her daily life and passes into the world of acting. This vestibule includes a physical warm-up in which the actor relaxes and warms up his or her voice and body and—more important—a mental warm-up in which the actor recognizes and honors the task he or she is about to undertake. It's the place where

25

you take off your boots and brush off the dust of your daily life before you get into your art. It is the vestibule of preparation.

THE PURPOSE OF PREPARATION

You are embarking on a very important work, a holy work, when you embark on the work of acting, for the merchandise you are dealing with is truth. You want to prepare for and approach that work as reverently and alertly as possible. But the main purpose of going into the vestibule is to prepare yourself so that you, the actor, will enjoy the experience of acting to its fullest. Only then will you best benefit your audience.

ALWAYS TAKE THE TIME

I don't believe in spending a lot of time in the vestibule, however (or lots of time doing either emotion or sense exercises, for that matter), because the crux of acting is relating with others, which happens only in scene work. I believe instruction should center on helping the actor learn how to get right to the heart of the conflict and resolution that constitute the soul of the scene. But to become calm and centered and focused on the work at hand, you do have to take a conscious and reverent moment to pass through the vestibule on the way to your acting work.

But what if we're in a hurry? We have five minutes to get home from work, take a shower, get dressed, and drive forty minutes to our audition or performance. How are we going to find the time to warm up? After all, isn't warming-up something of a luxury? We don't have time to do many things that are important to us. We don't have time to eat well. We don't have time to meditate. We don't have time to do our physical workouts. We certainly don't have the few minutes that it takes to go into the vestibule and prepare ourselves before we act. Right? Wrong! All of it. We *do* have the time. Despite appearances to the contrary, we always have time to do the right thing. As Einstein showed us, time is relative; it expands as we use it appropriately. Time's function is to support right activity, in the same way that place exists to support presence. If we take the time to prepare ourselves to act, not only will we find that we have enough time, we will also discover that we have gained time because now we will be working more effectively.

THE PHYSICAL AND THE MENTAL WARM-UP

The vestibule of preparation consists of two parts: the physical warm-up, during which you warm up the body and drop the tension, and the mental tune-up, during which you bust inhibitions that are the mental counterpart to the physical constrictions you are holding in your body. The physical warm-up and relaxation is tremendously helpful in preparing the actor to act. But even more important is achieving the mental and emotional relaxation and focus the actor needs before beginning to work.

✹ *Affirmation*

> *I am ready, willing, and able now, and I know that no one is more talented, smarter, better, or luckier than I am.* (See The Law of Luck in chapter 17.)

SAMPLE PHYSICAL AND MENTAL WARM-UPS

Below are a few examples of how you might best use your time in the vestibule.

▦ **The Five-Minute Five-Step Prep** (standing or sitting)

1. **Baby cries.** Take a deep breath and then, deep down, from your diaphragm, cry out "waah" as if you are a hungry little baby unself-consciously wailing for its nourishment. Do it three times. On the third become impatient, angry even, and pulse out the wail: "Wa-ah-ah!"

2. **Find the center.** Find the soft, sweet place of privacy in your consciousness and mentally place it somewhere in your body—your chest, solar plexus, or bowels. Breathe deeply into that place and focus your attention there, calming and centering yourself more deeply with each full breath. Do it five times.

3. **Relax and go limp.** Keeping your breathing slow and constant, do a slow neck roll, first to the left, then to the right. Then, in the following order, tighten and release your face, shoulders, arms, hands, back, and legs: tighten the muscles and hold them taut for ten seconds, then drop, shake, and relax them.

4. **Five consonants.** This is a vocal warm-up. Choose five consonants, for example K, L, B, D, R. Place a wine cork between your teeth and then, speaking as clearly as possible, speak loudly the five vowels, preceded by each of the consonants: kay, kee, ki, ko, ku; lay, lee, lie, lo, lu, and so on.

5. **Repeat step 2.** Find the center. Breathe deeply into that place and focus your attention there, calming and centering yourself more deeply with each full breath. Do it five times, then end it with a short prayer that acknowledges the importance of, and your ability to do, the work you are now about to undertake.

▦ **The Ten-Minute Five-Step Prep**
The above exercise, twice as long (which the five-minute version will unintentionally be, anyway, until you develop the skill to execute it efficiently).

▦ **The Chair Caveman-Emote Relaxation** (sitting)
Sit in an armless straight-back chair. Starting from the head down, tighten, hold, shake, and relax all major muscle groups (head and neck, shoulders, arms and hands, back and abdominals, buttocks, and legs and feet). At the same time, pretend that you are a caveman or -woman and using deep breathes and loud wordless vocalizations express at least five major emotions, such as fear, anger, joy, love, and envy. Translated into sounds, they might sound like "aah!" (fear), "ehh-yehh-yehh!" (anger), "ooh!" (joy), and so on.

▦ **The Audition Chair Grounding** (sitting)
This is a short, almost silent warm-up that you can do while you are sitting in the waiting room before your audition. Find yourself a corner. You won't be invisible, but neither will you be the center of attention.

Breathing deeply, slowly massage with your fingertips the muscles of your face (jaws, temples, forehead), the back of your neck, and your shoulders. Then extend your arms out sideways, shoulder height, leave them there until they burn, then cross them across your chest until you are hugging the opposite shoulders. Open them up and cross them the other way, again hugging the opposite shoulders.

Next, extend and tighten the muscles in your legs. Release. Flex your feet. Release. Rotate your ankles. Then fold your torso down until it is lying over your thighs, your hands on the ground, your head hanging limp between your knees. Breathe deeply. Slowly roll up.

Then, almost silently, hum to yourself either a peaceful tune or a single note that ends, then restarts, with each new breath. Do ten breaths. Then smile and say a little prayer, which includes gratitude that your audition can't help but be successful.

▦ Full-Body Chakra-Release Relaxation (lying down)

Lie on your back on a mat or towel. Breathe deeply, holding each inhalation for ten seconds before releasing. Do it three times.

Then begin a two-part process for each area of the body. You will first inhale and, working up progressively beginning with your feet, tighten specific muscles and hold them taut while you formulate a mental stance that relates to the energy center or chakra associated with that physical area. Then express your commitment to that stance by making an appropriate sound on exhaling. Begin with your feet alone.

1. **Feet.** Inhale and tense your feet. While holding them tight, think of something that grounds you. Let's say it's taking a walk. Then, on the exhalation/relaxation release, express by the sound you make when you exhale how you feel when you are grounded.

2. **Legs.** Inhale and tense your feet and legs. Think of something you stand for. Say it's the fact that you can achieve your dreams. Then on the release, express with the audible exhalation of your breath that you do, indeed, stand for that.

3. **Abdominals and buttocks (power/sex chakra).** Inhale and tense your feet, legs, abdominals, and buttocks. Think of something you desire and demand to have. It could be great success as an actor as well as spiritual illumination. On the release of the breath and the muscle tension, express that you do, indeed, want and demand to have it.

4. **Chest (heart chakra).** Inhale and tense your feet, legs, abdominals, buttocks, and chest muscles. Think of something you love. It could be your child, acting, puppy dogs, or chocolate ice cream. Be sure that by your exhalation it can be heard that you do, indeed, love it.

5. **Back.** Inhale and tense your feet, legs, abdominals, buttocks, chest, and back. Think of something you fully support. Maybe it's your lover or the work of some organization or an idea whose time has come. Let it be obvious that you do fully support it when you exhale/ release.

6. **Arms.** Inhale and tense your feet, legs, abdominals, buttocks, chest, back, arms, and hands. Think of something that you thoroughly embrace. Perhaps it's the idea that God is love, or that your own efforts are innocent and worthy. Whatever it is, audibly express by your exhalation release that you fully embrace it.

7. **Throat (throat chakra).** Inhale and tense your feet, legs, abdominals, buttocks, chest, back, arms, hands, neck, and throat. Think of something that you have to say. This is your message to the world, your voice, your statement. Maybe it's "don't worry; be happy," "you can do it," "it's never too late," or, as Ringo Starr used to say, "Don't get *real* with me!" When you release your muscles and breath, let your message, and the fact that you really mean it, be clearly audible.⁻

8. **Face.** Inhale and tense your feet, legs, abdominals, buttocks, chest, back, arms, hands, neck, throat, and face. In your mind complete this sentence: "I am _____." It could be I am perfect, pretty, successful, a good actor— anything that, in your heart of hearts, you know is true.

Release, and let it be heard in your exhalation your conviction that you are that.

9. **Head.** Inhale and tense your feet, legs, abdominals, buttocks, chest, back, arms, hands, neck, throat, face, and the back and top of your head. In your mind complete this sentence: "I know _____." It could be I know things are cool, I will make it, the truth, he loves me. Follow your instincts. But mean and commit to it. Then, on the exhalation, express that you truly know it.

Now lie silently for two minutes. Detach from all thought. When you find yourself thinking something, just detach and let the thought float by. Then slowly roll up to a sitting position, say a little prayer of gratitude and expectation of goodness, and come slowly to a standing position.

How do you feel? Don't even answer that. I know exactly how you feel. You feel fabulous! This exercise is also good whenever you are having a hard time falling asleep.

■ **The Ten-Minute Free-Form Relax Warm-Up**
This one you do your way.

ADDITIONAL WARM-UP SUGGESTIONS

The Yeah-Yeah Breath. Take a deep breath and pulse it out in short bursts by repeating the word *yeah* until the breath is gone. It's an affirmation as well as a breathing exercise. Do three of them.

Universal Hug. Reach up and open your arms to the universe to accept and embrace your good. Grab a large dosage of love, joy, success, and beauty; hug it to yourself and smile with gratitude.

Fake Laughter. Start out faking it until you begin to buy it. Feed it until it begins to feel natural and you are laughing your fool head off! It feels wonderful to the body and mind and is terrific proof that you are always in control of your emotions.

The Varying Ten-Breath Chant. Take in a breath, then release it using a sound pattern until the breath is gone. Inhale and exhale ten times, but each time use a different sound pattern on the exhale. If you are doing the chant with others, listen and relate to one another, but maintain your individuality.

Prayer. Pray your way.

※ EXERCISE

Try the above relaxation warm-ups to determine which ones work best for you, and then adopt the best ones for your personal use.

SUMMARY OF MAIN POINTS

1. The vestibule of preparation is the mental place where you "take off your boots" before you reverently embark upon the important work of acting. It includes the actor's physical warm-up.
2. Warming-up is neither a luxury nor too time consuming. Since it prepares the actor to work more efficiently and effectively, the actor actually gains time. We always have time to do the right thing.

CHAPTER 4

Representing a
State of Mind

Our calling is the art and craft of presenting a per-
sonality to an audience.

—Laurence Olivier

Now that we've looked at acting's relationship to our spiritual growth and explored where to get permission to do it and how to prepare to do it, let's look at what, in its essence, acting *is*.

At its core, acting is representing a state of mind. But what state of mind based on what standard? Supposedly there are, or have been, a few people (I don't personally know any of them) who are "pure." These saints, as the story goes, represent in human form the pure, unadulterated, good consciousness that we call God. I doubt that any of them live on my block, however. Certainly none of them are in my family, nor would anyone who knows me consider me one of them. The truth is, such souls are rarer than diamonds, which is not to say that they don't exist or that the rest of us are chopped liver. We're not; not pure chopped liver, anyway. Humans are beautiful but complex creatures who, from a relative perspective, are in the process of evolving.

THE IDEAL

We have been told by spiritual masters of every culture that we are representations of the being who created us, the offspring of God, or good. This is a cross-cultural consensus, and in our hearts we know it to be true. But this ideal seems far from our present experience. And yet, it's an ideal that we cherish and we aspire to. We think of our spiritual folk heroes or saints as having thought only good thoughts and successfully swatting away—as if playing some sort of spiritual badminton—each and every temptation to fall into any dark state of mind. Yes, they were the coolest, we think. They got every last bit of fear out of their consciousness before the heavens opened and swooped them up into some exclusive ongoing Mardi Gras. And when we're not aspiring to be mega movie stars or rock stars or professional basketball players, we see these saints as role models, the ones we really want to be like. There weren't many of them—Moses, Jesus, Buddha, a couple of women, probably, and a handful of others we'll never hear about. But that's about it. Hell, I suspect that not even that much is true. I suspect that everybody has had his or her stuff to work out, no matter how flawless history has painted him or her. Which leaves us with this realization: each man and woman is a psychic complexity— a complex combination of qualities and characteristics, some good and some bad. And when we as actors portray a man or a woman on stage, we are portraying a unique, complex state of mind.

✖ EXERCISE

Watch one of your favorite films that stars an actor or actress who reminds you of yourself. Watch until he or she has a two- or three-minute speech, a monologue. Replay it until you have written the monologue down. Another character may interrupt with a line or two, but eliminate those and improvise connecting lines until you've got a cohesive two- or three-minute speech. Now read it ten times. Then improvise the monologue. In other words, put it into your own words.

THE ACTOR'S BLUEPRINT

When you take on a part, you are given, in the form of the script, a blueprint for your character. In this blueprint the playwright gives you a list of materials (the qualities, emotions, actions, and words) and their quantities (degrees of those qualities, emotions, actions, and words) you need to create your character. But it is left to you, the actor, to build the character, and your materials are parts of yourself. Understanding and accepting this point is critical to understanding what acting is all about.

Writers create blueprints in words and actions—here's what your character says and does. But as an actor, you will have to go deeper than simply following the writer's blueprint; you will have to begin with what your character is first feeling and thinking, which will have come into being from his previous and unchronicled experience and will have gotten him to the point where he then says and does the things written by the playwright. Almost all of that, you, the actor, will have to create. Very rarely in play literature do you get from the playwright what a character is thinking, let alone what he's feeling. You get what he does and what he says—the facade of the house. You, the actor, create the interior, the living space, the heart and soul of the home. Your work, therefore, is to be a researcher, explorer, and builder. You have to figure out what this character is all about, so that you can then represent this particular state of mind on stage with full understanding, compassion, and commitment.

If the play is good, it will have an interesting selection of states of mind that interact with one another to convey the message of the play, a message that will be entertaining, informative, and inspiring. Your part in the collaboration is to live your character's state of mind on stage.

THE PSYCHIC SALAD

I find it helpful sometimes to think of the makeup of the characters I play or coach others to play as psychic salads. Each character, like we ourselves who create these characters, has his or her own individual combination of ingredients. Some characters have more green onion, others more tomato; some are a little light on the lettuce or heavy on the dressing. Let's take a look at some of the main ingredients that, in varying degrees, constitute this mental makeup. Each character is a mixture of:

1. Qualities and characteristics, such as industriousness, discipline, honesty.
2. Experiences, which constitute first-hand knowing.
3. Beliefs, which include unconscious beliefs, such as those that constitute the religious and political belief systems of a character's parents, as well as the conscious beliefs that he or she personally accepts for him- or herself.
4. Fears and insecurities.
5. Confusion and contradictions: conflicting beliefs and desires; inconsistencies that mark the human condition and are crucial to understanding a character.
6. Insights: those moments of understanding that, when they occur for a character, are the sparkling diamonds that light up the eyes of the audience.

7. Strengths and weaknesses: the degree to which a character is effective in executing his or her intentions or desires.
8. Virtues and faults.
9. Joy and sadness: the degree to which an individual can attain and sustain the state of joyfulness.
10. Success or failure: The degree to which one meets his or her objectives. Like strengths and weaknesses, virtues and faults, and joy and sadness, success and failure are the two poles of the positive quality—in this case, success. A character will be somewhere between the two poles. Thomas Edison defined success as "Being able to go from failure to failure without loss of enthusiasm!"

✖ EXERCISE

Please list ten good or bad qualities that, on a regular basis, you feel you employ and/or are known for employing among the *supportive* members of your family and friends.

1. _____	6. _____
2. _____	7. _____
3. _____	8. _____
4. _____	9. _____
5. _____	10. _____

Analyze the above. Do you like what you have come up with? Want to keep it as is or modify your "character" in some way? Stanislavski pointed out that the artist can draw only on what he has made of himself to build his characters.

As actors then, we represent these combined states of mind, these mixtures, that evolve throughout the unfolding events of the play. And we display them as faithfully, objectively, and non-judgmentally as we can so that the man and the woman in the audience, also complex individuals consisting of controversy, inconsistency, and contradiction, might experience a moment of true awakening and say, "Yes, that is truth; that is how it is; that is how I am," or he is, or she is, and might benefit and grow by the light of that truth.

❀ *Affirmation*

> *I am a life expert. I have the insight and ability to decipher and deliver for an audience the essence of any state of mind, or point of view that shall constitute my character.*

Our first task as actors, then, when taking up any part, is to thoroughly define and understand the makeup of the particular psychology that we have the honor of portraying.

❊ EXERCISE

Please write a short prayer for your own prosperity using statements that you are either certain are already true or wish to be true.

_____

_____

SUMMARY OF MAIN POINTS

1. In its essence, acting is representing a state of mind with full understanding, compassion, and commitment.
2. Each man and woman is a psychic complexity.
3. The actor is given, in the form of a script, only a blueprint for his or her character. It is left to the actor to build the character. The materials for the construction consist entirely of parts of the actor.

4. The actor portrays individual "psychic salads": unique combinations of good and bad qualities and characteristics that constitute characters who, like us, are works in progress.
5. A good play consists of an ensemble of different states of mind that interact with one another throughout the play to illustrate the play's message, which, when well constructed and well acted, will entertain, inform, and inspire the audience.

CHAPTER 5

The Emotional Journey

*Acting is the easiest job I could have had. I'm really
lucky to have this outlet for my feelings. Sometimes
I release my deepest, most hidden feelings by pretending to be someone else. It's wonderful.*

—Gregory Peck

It sounds quite grandiose and impressive and wonderful to say
that what you, as an actor, contribute to society is so valuable and worthwhile. Well, it *is* magnificent, and you are entitled to realize that it is and reap the benefits from it. And while
it is wonderful and worthy of great honor and respect, it also
fits easily within your achievement envelope. In fact, it's really
no big deal for you at all. It's natural to you. It's what you do,
because what you are doing as an actor is just living life. But
you are living it *on stage*. The trick is to live it as fully *on* stage
as you live it when *off* stage.

Defining and living the emotions appropriate to your character is natural because, by the time you are five years old, you
have already experienced all the major emotions, including
avarice, envy, sexuality, delight, pride, fear, and love. You, the
actor, are a life expert. There is no one more expert in life, no

one better at understanding and feeling any of life's emotions than you. You are a living human being, the real thing, the very thing you are portraying. Every bit of casting, therefore, provided they are casting a human being to portray a human being, is 100 percent dead-on perfect casting, and you the actor have the right to know and claim that fact for yourself. You are an expert man or woman, and you must honor your own personal expertise. That expertise is your calling card, your backstage pass, and the proof of your value as an artist.

What sets acting apart from most other occupations, including the other arts, is that acting's sole purpose is to elucidate the truth via each character's emotional journey. You may say that actors also want to entertain. But entertainment is just a carrier, a means for delivering the message and making the journey pleasant. It's the emotional journey that's important, for during that journey the character does, or does not, learn the lessons that, by watching him, his audience surely does.

◉ Affirmation

My intelligence and creative ability are as great as those of anyone who has ever lived.

THE TRIP

Every piece of theatrical literature, whether it's a screenplay or a stage play, maps out an emotional journey for each of its characters. And if it's a well-structured play, there will be good, cohesive, satisfying reasons why some characters, or states of mind, traveling perhaps on widely disparate paths at the journey's beginning will converge at the end, while other characters who seem to have been traveling along the same path will diverge. One thing is certain. Whether the playwright is a good cartographer or not, it is the responsibility of the actor to make sure that his or her character follows a lucid emotional path that starts out and resolves—or doesn't—and that the reasoning behind the progress and resolution or lack thereof is cogent and understandable to the audience.

Below is a list of emotions and emotional states to remind you of the many feelings we have—often several at once.

anger	grief	sadness
confidence	fear	sexiness
generosity	irritability	happiness
light-heartedness	hatred	shyness
compassion	insecurity	self-pity
conceit	jealousy	silliness
confusion	kindness	gratitude
contentment	love	stubbornness
courage	madness	surprise
depression	meanness	stupidity
moodiness	embarrassment	naughtiness
worry	envy	prejudice
self-doubt	pride	impatience
quarrelsomeness	resentment	hope

✖ EXERCISE

This is a four-part exercise:

Part I. Select six emotions that seem quite different from one another:

1. _____ 3. _____ 5. _____

2. _____ 4. _____ 6. _____

Part II. Recall and jot down in a very few words a time when you felt each of these emotions. (Examples: I felt envy when Mary won the spelling bee; I felt worry when my cat was lost; and so on.)

1. _____ 4. _____
2. _____ 5. _____
3. _____ 6. _____

Part III. One at a time, practice remembering the incident in Part II, and then feeling the emotion in Part I that it gave rise to. Progress from 1 through 6, then jump around: remember and feel the number 3 incident and emotion, for instance, then number 5.

Part IV. Now join them. Remember and feel number 1, then change to remembering and feeling number 2. Continue adding until you have built an emotional journey that includes all six of them and you are able, within one minute, to begin with number 1, then change to number 2, then number 3, and so on. When you feel you have achieved emotional fluidity, during which, like changing channels on your television set, you can add or easily change from one memory/emotion to another, you have finished.

Congratulate yourself! This is a major acting achievement!

THE BIG GOAL

As did our spiritual folk heroes, we, too, are working toward a sense of peace, joy, and love in our lives. We would like that to be our final mental and emotional destination at the end of our life's journey on Earth. We would like to reach it *now*, as a matter of fact, and be able, henceforth, to reside in that state of mind and enjoy life from that perspective, wouldn't we? But, as yet, we still seem to embody a conflicting combination of many emotions and our own journey in life consists of working through the negativity that would keep us from experiencing that bliss.

Like us, each of the characters we portray is on an emotional journey of his or her own. All these characters want the same things we do, including the highest ideals. That's because we are portraying people. We're going to portray only a slice of a character's life and only selected events within that slice. But regardless of which slice and which events within it, among our character's main objectives and desires will be his or her deepest desire for peace, joy, and love—because that is how people *are*.

"Acting is living on stage," said Stanislavski. As in life, so shall it be on stage. Since love is the highest emotional choice in life and bliss the deepest desire, so it is when working on stage. I have seen the acceptance of this truth to be the very thing that finally seats the character into place for an actor when he was having difficulty finding the character, because that deep desire is the truest one in every person and, therefore, in every character.

In life we say a person has grown or progressed if he or she has either achieved a greater degree of joy, peace, or love than he or she possessed before, or has rid his or her consciousness of the negative emotions that had polluted or conflicted it. Every dramatic adventure deals with elements of the same conflicts and challenges we meet every day. The dramatic adventure by definition is one in which desire is met by conflict and which then progresses toward some form of resolution. That is the human drama—both in life itself as well as on the stage that portrays it. From the spiritual perspective, this drama consists of a sense of dissatisfaction (desire) and the efforts and actions employed to alleviate that dissatisfaction or fulfill that desire, met by obstacles that reside only within the consciousness of the hero, which he then grows to resolve to some degree between total failure and total success—the degree dependent on the hero's success in mastering those fearful obstacles in himself. We, the audience, measure the degree of success by how happy the character is at the end: by how much peace, joy, and love are flying around and chirping like happy little birds in his consciousness, even if he didn't "get" what he thought he was going after.

DRAWING THE EMOTIONAL MAP

You as an actor have the task of deciphering the map of your character's emotional journey—much of which you will have to create and supply yourself—until you are clear about where your character is and is going. Your job is not finished—it's not even properly begun—until you have determined his desires and motives, which come from a cohesive history and belief system that you will have combined to create his state of mind at the beginning of the play. You will then complete the job by following through with a believable evolution of the character as he proceeds along on his journey, faces his challenges, and comes to a resolution, which may or may not prove "successful."

Ideally, you should be able to map out on a piece of paper, like a graph of highs and lows, the feelings that your character experiences along the way. And then, without words, using only sounds (an instrument like a kazoo, just your breath, or even moaning sounds), you should be able to express the emotions encountered as you proceed along the path of your character's journey. Try it. You will find it tremendously freeing.

Remember, drama is a collaborative art. You cannot expect the playwright to have provided everything. If he or she had done so, there would be no need for a director, actors, or the audience. So you must know and do your part as an actor, which, interestingly, just happens to be the most well-paid part. Star actors are the highest paid production members. This gives us a good reason to believe that acting must be the most important part of a production, which I believe it is, and not just because stars draw an audience. First, you must have a good story. Without that, you have nothing. But in drama, the words remain on the page until the actor contributes his body, mind, soul, and experience to make that story live for an audience.

THE ACTOR'S TOOL KIT

When I work with a new student who is attempting to map out his character's emotional journey, I first outfit the student for the task: "First lay out the blueprint for the play," I tell him, "then put on your overalls and your miner's hat with the light on it, then get out the two main acting tools from your actor's tool kit." According to Grandpa Stanislavski, those tools are the actor's experience and imagination. Then, and only then, do you go to work.

Experience and imagination. They are the two main tools in any actor's tool kit. And of the two, experience is the more important and powerful because your imagination is a mental extension of your experience—which is not a slight to your imagination, nor does it contradict Einstein's statement that "imagination is more important than knowledge." Knowledge and experience are two different things. Experience is the undeniable, personal realization of reality, whereas knowledge resides in an intellectual space that is not necessarily experiential.

✖ EXERCISE

Please imagine and describe below the wildest chair that you can think of. Really let it rip. Imagine first a white background and then, in front of that, place your chair.

You might have envisioned the chair seat as the flat extended tongue of a monster, or imagined a giant Venus flytrap chair that scooped you up when it sensed you were tired and then swayed you gracefully in the air. But I'll bet that whatever the design, your wild chair was based on your past experience of "chair." So your experience, which makes you an expert, is

47

honorable and your most effective tool to help you relate to and relax into your character.

PUTTING THE TOOLS TO USE: CHARTING THE JOURNEY

Now that we have our blueprint, our expertise, and our tools, we are ready to chart the emotional journey our character is about to embark on. There are four steps in charting a character's emotional journey.

1. The first thing we do is "fly over it." We first overview and explore the complex state of mind that the playwright gives us in the form of a blueprint in actions and words. You just check it out, staying objective and noncommittal.

2. Second, we zoom in to the specific important moments within the drama, then to the less important ones that both lead up to and result from the bigger moments. These are the peaks and valleys. Identify, name, and define each specific emotion along each step of the drama: "When she's doing this she is feeling envy; when she is saying that, she is feeling self-consciousness." Write these emotions down in the right margins of the text in red ink.

3. Third, using your two main tools of experience and imagination, find ways within yourself to personally identify with those feelings. Translate the point of view from the third person to the first person and identify with every aspect of it: "Yes, I felt like that the time my sister did so and so to me. I felt like *that* when they all turned and looked at me." Write those correspondences down in the left margins in blue. It may not be the exact same experience—how could it be?—but, with the aid of your imagination, it will be close enough to help you empathize with what the character is meant to be feeling. You should do this work thoroughly until you feel that you've got it.

4. Fourth, actually graph the journey. Up will represent the emotions that are more blissful or desirable to our character,

and down will represent the less satisfying, darker emotions, the states of mind with more anxiety and other junk in them. The graph will give you a good, objective overview of your character's emotional journey within the framework of the play. You'll be able to see, for instance, that during Act I she's down most of the time, then up a bit in Act II, then down half of Act II, but up at the end. And you'll know *why*—all of which will increase your insight and make you, the actor who is playing her, feel more confident.

FOLLOWING THE MAP

Once you have charted your course, you have to provide from within yourself the emotions and thoughts that lie beneath and precede the words and actions given you by the playwright. Notice that when you have something to communicate, first, you feel it; second, you put your feelings into thoughts; and third, you express your feelings and thoughts verbally as words. Emotions lead to thoughts; thoughts lead to words and actions.

My communication, therefore, in life and onstage, begins and ends not with the words themselves, but with the expression of emotion. Even before I use words, if you are in the room with me and are the least bit discerning, you will already have begun to receive my communication. And when the communication comes out as words, if my words are true to my thoughts and feelings, you will have fully received my communiqué.

However, I do have the ability to lie. If at any time I choose to think something in contradiction to my feelings (which in psychology is called neurosis), or to say something opposite to those feelings, so that my feelings, thoughts, and words are not true to one another, you will become confused or suspicious. In acting, therefore, where communication *of* the point *is* the point, unless your character is meant to be lying, it is incumbent upon you, the actor, to be clear and consistent in the feelings, thoughts, and actions of your character.

A well-written play is structured so that the journey of each character crosses paths with other characters at specific emotion points. For that to work most effectively in furthering the message of the play, each actor must be consistent and cohesive in making and expressing his or her emotional choices and careful that they are in concert with the words and actions he or she is given by the playwright so that the communication received by the audience is clear and understood as intended.

✖ EXERCISE

Part I. Pretend you are a big star and are being interviewed for an important magazine. Answer the following questions. There's a catch, however: Everything that you say must be a lie!

1. How did you become famous?

_____

_____

2. Why did you want to be a star?

_____

_____

3. What did you have to sacrifice, or give up, to be a star?

_____

_____

4. What are the most important things in your life now?

_____

_____

5. If you had it all to do over again, what would you do differently?

_____

_____

6. What advice do you have for a young actor who is trying to make it today?

_____

_____

Remember now, everything you write must be a lie!

Part II. Ask a friend to interview you, using the questions listed in Part I. Tape record the questions and your responses. Don't tell your friend that you are lying. Play it straight; don't laugh or come off your position, regardless how your interviewer reacts. When it is over and you have your answers and your interviewer's reactions on tape—which will be very interesting for you to review later—then you can tell him the truth, if you must!

In my classes and workshops, I have two students go up before the class for this exercise. Before the exercise begins, I privately instruct one of them to lie and the other to tell the truth. Then I ask the students in the audience to identify who is telling the truth and who is "the dirty lying star." They must determine the differences between how the two actors, the liar and the truth-teller, act and how much truth the lying actor unwittingly reveals. The point of this exercise for you, the "liar," is to experience how different it feels to lie when fear is not the motivation from lying motivated by fear (which is usually when we lie in life) or telling the truth.

SUMMARY OF MAIN POINTS

1. What you, as an actor, contribute to society is natural for you. You are simply living life on stage. You are a life expert, an expert on the very thing that you are portraying—a person.

2. You, as a character, take an emotional journey from one state of mind at the play's opening to another at the end.

3. Acting is living on stage. Just as love is the highest emotional choice in life and bliss the deepest desire, so they are in the life of your character.

4. If the play has value and serves you and the audience by accurately rendering the truth, which enlightens the dark corners of the psyche and alleviates suffering, its contribution is extremely valuable.

5. The playwright provides the words and the actions. You, the actor, supply the emotions, thoughts, motives, and ulterior motives—all the mental and emotional complexities that precede and motivate those words and actions.

6. You should be able to chart your character's emotional journey on a sheet of paper as follows: (1) see the journey from overviewing the play as a whole; (2) zoom in on each notable moment in the play; (3) find ways to personally identify with each moment that impacts your character; and (4) graph your character's emotional ups and downs. To do this, use the two main tools in an actor's tool kit: experience and imagination.

7. It is important for you, the actor, to be clear and consistent in your feelings, thoughts, and actions so that the audience will understand them without confusion.

CHAPTER 6

The Almighty Armchair

Inner characterization can be shaped only from an actor's own inner elements. If this is effectively prepared, the outer characterization should naturally follow.

— Constantine Stanislavski

Where do you do this mental and emotional exploration that leads to inner characterization, plus identify, define, and then identify *with* the specifications of your character and make those choices that lead eventually to the outer characterization? You do it in your "almighty armchair."

The armchair. It's a rocking chair, a Lay-Z Boy recliner, an overstuffed velvet chair. It is any comfortable chair that has arms so that you can slouch in it and throw your legs over it and sit and think and explore the work that you are about to undertake as an actor. I call it the *almighty* armchair because worlds are created there. It is the place that hosts your bum while you travel into the world of your character. It's the place where you discover what's in the text as well as discover and create the subtext, do your mental and emotional research, create your character's biography—both past *and* future—and take your character's emotional journey for the first time. And before you later take that journey many times on stage, you will have first taken it many more times in your armchair. It is the place where you first live—so that your character can later relive them onstage—the stories that your character will be telling.

PRELIVING THE STORY: CREATING THE MAN-MADE LAKE

Let's say that my character has to tell a story that goes something like this: "The other day I was playing tennis at the Beach Club and I met a man who looks exactly like Clark Gable and all of a sudden a tiny flying saucer, no bigger than a tennis ball, landed on his head." I, the actor, am faced with the task of telling a story of something that happened in my character's past, but it didn't happen to me. And if it didn't happen to me—if I didn't experience it—I can't make it happen for my character.

But if I sit in my armchair and imagine, in detail, this story really happening—imagine myself going to a specific tennis court on a specific day at a specific time with specific weather and imagine what I was wearing and how I was feeling that day and what I first saw when I arrived and how I met the Clark look-alike and the interchange we had, and so on—then I create that "reality" in my mind. It will not be a *real* reality, any more than a man-made lake would be a real lake, but the construction—because the imagination is as suggestible to fantasy as to fact—*will* hold water. When I get up on stage to tell this story, my subconscious will have registered a certain veracity about the events. It will seem as real to my subconscious as many of my real experiences. After all, I will have experienced it, if only in my imagination, in my armchair. And working this way will give me enough conviction that the audience will buy it without blinking an eye.

※ EXERCISE

Find a play in which the character relates a story. First live the story in your mind in detail, then memorize the lines and relive the story when you recite them.

If you don't want to do the homework, however, if you don't want to create a biography for your character and the between-the-lines subtext, if you don't want to take the time to read the text ten times before you begin to work on it and think about it deeply for hours—all of which happens in your armchair—then you don't want to be an actor. Because most of your acting, like most of an iceberg, occurs behind or beneath the scenes; only the tip of the iceberg appears above the water, and only the apex of the acting work—the performance—appears on stage. But the performance is built in your armchair, and then later during rehearsals.

BEING THOROUGH

If you do want to act, however, and are willing to do the work, you will find that there is nothing stressful in doing your armchair work. What is stressful is *not* doing the work that you know you should, because then you're going to have to get up and perform when you know that you're not prepared. *That's* stressful! But if you do your preparation, when you get up on stage nothing will topple you. You'll be on a solid foundation of knowing where you are and what you are doing during each phase of the emotional journey that your character is taking.

AVOID THE TEMPTATION TO MEMORIZE

There is one thing it is important *not* to do: memorize your lines too soon. Doing this is one of the biggest mistakes that an actor can make. You do not get the cookie in acting for knowing your lines. You may get it in third grade for knowing the "Star-Spangled Banner," or how to spell Beelzebub, but you do not get it for memorization in acting. In acting, you get the cookie for feeling the feelings. That's what we hire you to do, that's what we each give you our ten (or a hundred and ten) bucks for—so that right there, on the spot, you will actually take the emotional journey for us. Resist the temptation to memorize quickly so that you can "perform"—which is nothing but artistic self-indulgence if you're not yet prepared to perform. First do your work thoroughly in your armchair so that you can intelligently decide how you want to deliver your lines and, therefore, how to memorize them, and you will be doing your work as an actor. Because the part of the mind that memorizes is a copy machine, and if you copy your lines before putting them into proper emotional alignment, what have you gained? You've copied them out of place, and it's now going to be much harder for you to rearrange them.

Instead, in your armchair thoroughly figure out what the hell's going on with your character, why he's saying what he's saying and what he really means. *Then* begin to memorize his words. If you will do that, you will have avoided the anxiety that usually comes with memorizing. Plus you'll discover, when you're ready to memorize them, that you already have most of them memorized anyway. You will also be less likely to forget your lines working this way because you will know your emotional journey—you'll know you're feeling up here, down there—and the lines will more obviously express those ups and downs. Even if you do forget your lines, you will be better able to improvise or vamp in place, which will lessen your chances of being afflicted by that blinding mental horror we call stage fright.

VAMPING

By the term *vamping* I mean "dancing in place." It's like treading water; it keeps you afloat but it doesn't further your action. It's a tremendously comforting tool to have at your disposal because there's nothing scarier than when you're on stage and you suddenly forget your lines. The essence of the technique is that you simply talk more about what you just said.

Let's say I'm doing a monologue and the text is as follows: "You know, I was at the market yesterday and I ran into Bob Thompson. You know, the guy who sells Buicks over on the boulevard? Well, Bob told me that he knows a place where you can buy three- to five-carat diamonds for five hundred dollars a carat! And they're good quality, too! So I got this idea. I figured, if you and I went in together, we could open a little jewelry shop right here in town and make a quick killing! What do you think?"

OK, that's my monologue. And I'm rolling along: "Well, Bob told me that he knows a place where you can buy three- to five-carat diamonds for five hundred dollars a carat! . . ." and this is where I forget my lines. So, I vamp; I stay right where I am and just talk a little more about what I just said, something like: "Only five hundred dollars! Isn't that amazing?! I mean, have you ever heard of a price that low?" And now, magically, I remember my cue: "And they're good quality, too!" And I continue along.

This little trick works because the mind is so wonderful! And if you will occupy the part of the mind that is freaking out, going "Oh, my God! Oh, my God!," by simply continuing to talk about what you have already said, then the part of the mind that is secure and knows what is happening will lead you to say a word or a phrase (in this case, "a price that low") that will trigger your memory and lead you right back on track ("And they're good quality, too!"). Not only will you find yourself back on track, you will find that your landing is charged with an extra-emotional kick that punches up the excitement in the scene, which you will have earned by having been thorough in your armchair preparation work.

I remember hearing Alfred Hitchcock say that he made his films before he ever set foot on the sound stage. He mapped them out, knew exactly how he wanted to shoot and cut them, then went and filmed what he had first thoroughly outlined in his mind. Hitchcock was an artist with craftsmanlike artistry. His preparation didn't rob him of spontaneity. On the contrary, it freed him to employ and enjoy it. The same goes for you as an actor. You have a job to do—a big job. And big jobs take lots of hard and *smart* work.

⊛ *Affirmation*

I delight in being thoroughly prepared and am willing to do the work to become so.

YOUR ARMCHAIR INCLUDES IT ALL

Although acting is a collaborative effort when performed for an audience, you can "act" at any time because the heart and soul of acting is built in the actor's armchair. You're not dependent on an ensemble of cast and crew, theater space, backers, or an audience. At any time you can get a piece of text—a monologue, perhaps—sit down in your armchair, figure out what's going on, and start dealing with it. And when you do that, you are acting. You begin to become an actor the moment you sit your butt down in your armchair with a piece of text and begin. Why not begin right now? Who knows what heights you'll reach.

SUMMARY OF MAIN POINTS

1. The almighty armchair is where you do your research and break down the components of the play. It is where you first live, so that you can later relive, the stories your character will relate. It is where you create your character's past, present, and future.
2. Only you, the actor, can give life to a character.
3. Never memorize too soon. The part of the mind that memorizes is a copy machine, and memorizing lines before they are in proper emotional alignment defeats the actor's purpose of feeling the appropriate feelings for an audience.
4. Being thorough in your armchair work lessens your chances of being afflicted by stage fright or forgetting your lines.

CHAPTER 7

Imbibing the Character

What you ought to look for in choosing someone for a part is whether or not that person can play and is right for the highest moment in the part.

—Robert Lewis

We were encouraged by our parents and instructors when we were children to imbibe the characteristics of our heroes and our God. We are encouraged to do so still—if only by ourselves. What this means is that the child is encouraged to become his or her best; but not to become something other than what he or she is. No one can become something he or she is not.

An actor, however, is often given a confusing message when he is asked to imbibe the character he is playing: he is told to "become the character." "Oh, my God, I've got to become the character!" he frets and with good reason. "I've got to stop being me and become someone else!" That, you've got to admit, would definitely be hard to pull off. And trying to do so is one of the main things that ruins an actor's experience. "I've got to become the character!" As if a carrot has got to become a turnip one day and then next season become a pickle! No wonder actors run screaming from the stage when presented with such an impossible expectation, or that those who stay ask the most common question about acting, "How do I become the character?"

Well, the shorthand answer is that you don't. You don't become the character. If anyone becomes anything, it is the character that, through your creating it, *becomes*, or comes into being. But you do not become the character. There. Now, doesn't that feel nice? You see, it is impossible for an actor to become the character because, until the actor brings the character into existence, there exists no character to become. What the actor is provided with via the stage or screenplay is merely a blueprint for the character. But the building of the character is the job of the actor who plays the character, and she constructs this character out of materials that reside within herself.

You do not have to become an already created character. I hope you will get much comfort from that. On the contrary, you will have to *create* the character when you are cast to *play* her by giving her your body, your voice, your mind, and your life experience. So you can relax.

There is no mystery to acting. Acting is, literally, the most natural thing in the world. It is simply you as the actor selecting and using elements in your psyche to a greater or lesser degree until you are satisfied that you have formulated the proper combination of mental ingredients at the right levels of intensity to make up the state of mind, or character, you are playing. To say that an actor must "become the character" is a mistake as confusing as the saying "the sun rises." When we say that the sun rises, we know that we don't really mean it. Please be clear about this falsehood, because the false notion that the actor has to become the character is one of the greatest causes of confusion and discomfort for actors.

❀ *Affirmation*

That which is, already is; nothing can be added to or taken away from it.

EXERCISE

Be an animal. Choose an animal that you love and have an affinity for. Let's say that you choose an eight-month-old golden retriever puppy. Sit on the floor—make sure there's some space around you in which you can work—and then, using your imaginary senses, envision the dog you are going to embody. Just watch this puppy in your mind for a moment. Then begin to mirror one of its actions—maybe it looks around sharply at a noise, then returns its attention to gnawing a bone. Alternate between simply watching it and mirroring its actions until you feel you are in the swing of it and you and the puppy are "one." Then let it bark. First listen, then echo it. Then frolic along in psychic puppydom for a few minutes, stopping to simply watch and listen to it for a few seconds if you lose your vision.

What did you learn? You learned that you could do it, for one thing. But what else? You learned that by using your experience and imagination you were able to create the character out of elements from within yourself.

IMBIBING FROM WITHIN

The definition of the word *imbibe* is "to soak up, to receive, to assimilate." When you begin to play a role, you soak up, receive, and assimilate the qualities, characteristics and experiences you select from your own mental storehouse for your character, as prescribed by:

1. **The author:** what the author tells you through the character description.
2. **The character:** what the character says within the play about him- or herself.
3. **The other characters:** what the other characters in the

play say to your character and to one another about your character.

4. **Your own instincts:** what you know from your own experience of yourself and others that informs you about the possibilities of who the character is.

These are the four main sources of information that will guide you when deciding which elements, and to what degree, to activate in your own psyche as you play the role.

Here's another way of looking at it. When you are playing a guitar, you press certain strings within certain frets along the neck of the guitar to make certain notes and chords. When you are imbibing a character, you select certain characteristics from your psyche to serve the message of the play.

Do you ever *lose* yourself to become a character, though? No. On the contrary, you *use* yourself, or parts of yourself. Actually, you use every bit of yourself to determine which specific facets of yourself you want to employ. And if there are experiences outlined by the playwright that you have not personally had in your own life—which happens all the time—you call upon your own experience and imagination to find a way to relate as closely as possible to those prescribed experiences. This is where your own personal characteristics of compassion and empathy come in. You may not have been exactly there, but you have been somewhere close by, and the human heart is such that it understands.

Let's say, for example, that you're playing a child whose experiences seem very different from your own. Well, you can't lose your own experiences as a child, can you? Nor do you want to. You use your experience as a child to understand your character's experience as a child. If your character grew up in Kansas and you grew up in California, you add to your "factual" experience that you also grew up in Kansas and have another family. Then, in your preparation, you choose to think more about your new family. But you are always using your own experience to process and interpret the experiences of your character. It is from your own experience of life that you develop the compassion to understand the experiences of others, as well as the courage and conviction necessary to imbibe the experiences of your character. You determine how to play the character based on your experience of life. That's what makes you the expert on the characters you play. That's what makes you an artist. If you lined up ten actors to play a certain character, each would play the character differently. That's what casting is all about. When a director hires *you*, it is for *your* life expertise, which he or she believes will do the greatest justice to his or her vision of the play. So make sure that you do it your way.

※ EXERCISE

> Create a character and be that character all day. Write your character's one-page biography, giving him or her a past and a present, a name, and a main objective for the day. Then imbibe the character by selecting—accentuating and suppressing—certain characteristics of your own individuality. Note your observations.

YOU ARE ALWAYS THE STAR

You are always the star and your character is always the star character of the play. That is the position that I always encourage my students to take whether they have the lead role or a walk-on part. And I'll tell you why: "Acting is living on stage." That's your yardstick, the measuring rod by which we judge. In your own life you are the star, aren't you? Of course you are. One of us may be your leading man or leading lady, but the rest of us are extras in your life. You are the star in your life, and the rest of us, at best, are but supporting players. Since that is true in life, let it be so on stage!

A wonderful film by Francois Truffaut called *Day for Night* is a cinema verité drama about the making of a film. There is a segment in the film in which, one by one, the actors of the film within the film are interviewed by a documentary filmmaker. Shamelessly solipsistic, each one speaks from the point of view that his or hers is the lead character of the film. It was brilliant. It was meant to illustrate the so-called egocentricity of the actor, I think (which I, personally, do not subscribe to), but to me it illustrated a truth deeper, perhaps, than Truffaut may have even intended—that we each, in our own lives, *are* the star.

Try this out. The next time you are in a play—a stage play or a film play—approach the part from the standpoint that your character is the central character of the play and that the play, in fact, is about what's going on in the life of your character. This shift in perspective will enable you to more clearly perceive the interplay between the characters, because this point of view will be the most lifelike, and it will also be the most fun and rewarding for you.

Let's say you're doing a film that takes place in a supermarket and the central characters are the store manager and one of the female checkout clerks. In your role as an extra you go in, buy a jar of pickles, and leave. Although within the play itself it appears that your role is insignificant, I suggest that you as the actor not only can but *must* be a living example of that great statement, "There are no small parts." Do your part by living, with dignity, the fact that, hey, you have a life. That checkout clerk and store manager are insignificant to *you,* except for the fact that they will assist you in buying a jar of pickles. You have your present life, your prelife (the life before the scene), and your afterlife (the life after the scene). You, the star, go in, buy your pickles, and leave. You are feeling and thinking things when you go in, feeling and thinking things while you are there, and feeling and thinking things when you leave. Your character is not a small part of that supermarket scene; that supermarket scene is a small part of your character's day!

Now, if every actor, including every extra, would play his or her role with that sense of importance and responsibility and dignity, the scene would be crackling with life. It wouldn't be just an assemblage of empty-headed bodies passing in and out of frame, hitting marks, and rambling lines. If every role were played with that sense of not *egotistic* but *egoistic* responsibility, it would charge the play with such excitement and meaning that the delight that the audience would feel at witnessing such jam-packed aliveness would be orgasmic! Achieving that level of completeness is a function of direction more than anything else, of course, but as an actor you can't depend on direction from anyone else. You can depend only on doing your own good work.

Once you have established that your character is the central character in your play, begin to determine your character's relationship with each of the other characters, as well as the governing objectives that motivate them. These three things—considering yourself the star, understanding your character's relationship to the others in the play, and understanding what each of you want—will seat you comfortably in the reality of the play, because this analysis, which pivots around your self, is lifelike. Then your job is to focus on and achieve your character's motives and objectives.

EMOTIONAL ENUNCIATION

A good play is a symphony of emotions all interplaying and ultimately resolving toward a particular outcome of truth. And you must play your part, whether you're playing a good guy or a bad guy, with full commitment to your conscious choices— with *full emotional enunciation*—to serve that truth to the benefit of the audience.

Full emotional enunciation. What does that mean? If I ask you to enunciate your words clearly, I am asking you to say your words with more precision so that I can clearly hear them and interpret their meaning. When I ask you to play your part with *emotional* enunciation, I am asking you to *feel* more definitely and fully your character's emotions so I can more clearly and easily understand your character's point of view, especially what the character is feeling and thinking in relation to others in the play. As a character, you stand for a particular point of view that contrasts with others. You are not neutral. Society may encourage us to be neutral and quiet, to not be a troublemaker or draw attention to ourselves and disturb the established, reigning order, but that is not the case in drama. In drama we would lose interest in a character that was as bland as that. We would despise a character like that—as we often hate ourselves when we behave like some kind of wimpy, wishy-washy character. The point is, there is no fence-sitting in drama. Your character not only *takes*, he *is* a particular point of view. And by the time you are ready to perform it, you know your character's point of view inside out, *clearly*, and you *be* it. Because it is only by clearly being that note, that particular collective blend of emotional note, that the audience can see and understand your place in the emotionally symphonic drama. We're not talking about melodrama, which is acting like or pretending you feel more than you do. We're talking about truly feeling strongly in order to clearly play your part in elucidating the truth for your audience.

Once you have done all that—dubbed your own character "the star," understood all the characters' motives and objectives as well as their relationships between one another, and become committed to playing your part with full emotional enunciation—then, and only then, is the character truly your character. Then you have more than imbibed the character; you have created the character. The character has finally become, and what it has become is you.

SUMMARY OF MAIN POINTS

1. No one can become someone that he or she is not; therefore, an actor does not become the character. It is the character that *becomes* or comes into being through the actor's interpretive efforts.

2. There is no character until the actor brings the character into existence, using the materials of his or her self. The playwright merely provides the actor a blueprint for the character's construction.

3. An actor brings a character to life by selecting and activating elements within him- or herself. Four main sources of information guide the actor's choices: the playwright, the character's words about him- or herself, the other characters' words about the character, and the actor's own instincts.

4. An actor must play his or her part with full and clear emotional enunciation in order for the audience to reap full understanding. There is no fence-sitting in drama.

5. Considering his or her character the star of the play, understanding the relationships between the characters and what each character wants, and playing the part with full emotional enunciation securely seats the actor in the reality of the play; only then is the character truly the actor's character.

CHAPTER 8

The Qualities and Qualification of a Great Actor

Not only did I know that I was going to be an actress, I knew that I was going to be a great actress.
—Dame Judith Anderson

What are the qualities, or personal attributes, that make a great actor? Please take a moment to reflect on what it takes to perform convincingly.

THE QUALITIES

EXERCISE

Write down eight qualities that you think must be part of the psychological makeup of a great actor.

1. ________________	5. ________________
2. ________________	6. ________________
3. ________________	7. ________________
4. ________________	8. ________________

Did you list any of the following qualities?

insight	compassion	understanding
love	discipline	thoroughness
humility	devotion	dedication
honesty	concern	sensitivity
kindness	conviction	courage
versatility	commitment	sincerity
imagination		

I'm not surprised. You are a life expert, after all. Not only do you know what characteristics are present in a fine actor, I'm sure you can also see that the qualities that go into making a fine actor are the same ones that go into making a fine person and that you have all those characteristics yourself. The more the actor claims, activates, and cultivates these qualities and characteristics in himself, the more he has to draw on as an artist.

You have to be intelligent to be a fine actor. You have to have great insight and understand what's really going on with people—the interplay between the emotions, the subtleties within the interactions. You have to understand their desires, insecurities, fears, hopes, and disappointments. You must be sincere, courageous, and devoted to your craft. You must be honest with your feelings and be willing to expose and express them. And you must love even the worst of us.

Those are the qualities that make a great actor because they are the qualities that make a great person, and acting is simply being a person on stage, an artist in service to truth. The more you actualize your own spiritual magnificence, the more you will be able to apply that magnificence to your art for the greater benefit of your audience.

☸ Affirmation

I am as talented an actor as any actor who has ever lived.

WHAT QUALIFIES YOU TO BE AN ACTOR

EXERCISE

What qualifies one to be an actor? Write down the first answer that pops into your mind.

____

____

____

OK, I have a confession to make. That was a trick question. Because, as you'll note in the chapter title, I have used the singular word "qualification." I believe there is only one qualification to be an actor and that is, you have to be a person. If you're not a person, then give it up. You'll never make it. But if you are a human being living on this planet, you have everything that you need to be an actor. After all, what are you doing on stage? You are portraying a person, aren't you? You're a person, right? Well, all right, then! You're qualified.

I'm dead serious. Yes, we're going to need to learn acting technique—we need to learn technique in every area of expertise, including how to tie our shoes. But as far as the art of it goes—the heart of it, the spirit of it, the truth of it—anyone can be an actor. And, again, where do you get the permission to be one? You've already got it; it's God-given. And how do you activate it? You accept it, with gratitude.

Of course, an actor *does* have to have looks.

YOU'VE GOT TO HAVE LOOKS

Some people say that to be a successful actor, especially a movie star, you have to have looks, to which I say a truer word has never been spoken. I mean, how can you deny it? You do have to be *apparent*. If they point the camera at you and you are invisible like Dracula's image in a mirror, that's going to be a definite drawback. So, granted, you have to be able to be seen. But you *do* look like something, right? *You*, as a matter of fact. So, no problem. You've got looks.

An actor has to have looks, but those looks do *not* have to be "good" looks according to someone else's judgment. We don't even have to have all our appendages or all our faculties working to be a fine actor. But you do have to exist on this planet at this time and you have to be able to be perceived by others. Now, do you qualify? Great, then you're all set.

※ EXERCISE

List ten actors or actresses that, at first blush, do not seem to fit the popular description of a theater or film star.

1. _____   6. _____
2. _____   7. _____
3. _____   8. _____
4. _____   9. _____
5. _____   10. _____

Do you think you have less chance of being successful than these people had?

THE KEY TO BEING A GREAT ACTOR

Of all the human qualities, "the greatest of these," as St. Paul said, "is love." Not only is love the greatest characteristic of an individual, as well as his or her highest emotional choice, it is also the greatest asset the actor has at his or her disposal in drama. Love is the smartest choice for relating on and off stage because love keeps everything working together so that life continues to perpetuate itself.

How does this great asset serve us in our acting? Only love has the power to open our eyes and allow us to see clearly. When I choose to hate you because you did something "bad" to me, then I close down and see little. Hatred blinds me and limits my choices. But the moment I open up and decide to love, all of a sudden I am relieved of that agitating mental darkness. My vision clears and I am able to see what is really going on and what to do about it. On stage, this openness enables me to discover new opportunities and ideas about how to best play my role. Love puts us in our highest state of receptivity.

AN EXAMPLE OF HOW LOVE LIGHTS THE WAY

John Travolta in an interview on television told the story of how he got his role in Quentin Tarantino's film, *Pulp Fiction*. His career was going nowhere; he was getting no calls and was feeling very discouraged. Then one day in his spiritual work he progressed past discouragement to a place of true self-surrender. He prayed and said, "Maybe acting is not what I'm supposed to be doing now. Perhaps it's no longer my work," and he became willing to give it up if he could better serve in another area. Within the next twenty-four hours he received a phone call from Quentin Tarantino who asked him if he would consider playing the role in *Pulp Fiction*.

Travolta explained that if he had not been in that receptive state, which had come from his willingness to be an instrument of service, he might have said, "Quentin who? That little film? I'm a movie star! Forget it!" But because he was in a loving state of humble receptivity, he was able to recognize and accept the opportunity that came to him, which proved to be the catalyst for the resurgence of his career—a career that is now more successful than ever—not to mention the fact that, for his role in *Pulp Fiction*, he was nominated for the Academy Award for Best Actor.

When love is our standpoint in our acting work, our choices for our characters will be more intelligent and interesting. There's nothing more interesting—or villainous, for that matter—than a villain who comes to us with love in his or her eyes, for instance. And when we take love onto the stage with us, we will feel more secure, more spontaneous, and be better able to cooperate with the other actors in the play. Meryl Streep said, "The art of acting is in the actor's choices; everything else is technique, which you can learn." The highest choices come from the highest consciousness—love. Love is the key to great acting.

SUMMARY OF MAIN POINTS

1. Not only do we innately know what characteristics constitute a fine actor, each of us has all those characteristics.
2. A great actor must have great empathy for the human condition and love even the worst of us.
3. There is only one qualification you must meet to be an actor; you must be a person! Yes, you must learn acting technique and, yes, you have to have looks to be an actor. But you can learn it and you do look like something—you—so you're all set.
4. Just as love is the key to being a great person, love is the key to being a great actor, because love is the quality of mind that puts us in the highest state of receptivity.

Part II

HOW TO
DO IT

*Insight on
How to Work
More Effectively
on Your Craft*

CHAPTER 9

Finding Your System or Method

As in all Method training, each actor must find the parts of the Method that work for him; he follows his own "path to discovery."

—Lorrie Hull

THE ORIGIN OF THE THEATER

There are two main theories about how theater began. The first is that theater began as ritual. It was entertainment, yes, but it was directed toward appeasing the gods. The gods were the audience and the whole society performed. The people would get together and perform around a big campfire and ask the gods to give them a good harvest or make them fertile or prevent disaster such as drought or war with their neighbors. "History teaches us," said Rita Gam, "that the first actors were priests."

The second main theory is that the existence of dramatic narrative and storytelling is, and always has been, a natural, instinctive part of every man and woman since the beginning of time. It's simply a part of who we are. We want to talk, to relate our experiences to one another, to share and explain what has happened to us. This instinct helps us to make sense of what is happening in our own lives and, when we relate it, we help one another. Modern drama, as we know it today, is simply a more evolved and sophisticated way to accomplish those ends.

It is important for the actor to understand that theater has always existed in society and to accept, therefore, that theater is not a luxury. Theater is a necessity, a nonexpendable function of a healthy society. It exists to help us make sense of our experiences and grow.

THE HISTORY OF DRAMA

The first historical record of theater suggests that theater began formally in Greece some time between the eighth and sixth centuries BC. Drama was officially recognized in 534 BC in Athens, Greece, at the City Dionysia—a major religious festival honoring Dionysus. That year, a contest for the best tragedy was instituted at the festival and the winner was a man named Thespis. His play, it is surmised, was constituted of material drawn from mythology; that would not have been unusual. What made his play different and the first expression of drama was that Thespis directed an actor (the word *actor* derives from the word *answerer*) to speak all the lines. Not only did the actor speak the lines instead of singing them, which was the norm at that time, he spoke of events he had not personally experienced. This actor was neither appeasing the gods nor relating a personal experience. Rather, he pretended that the experiences he was relating had been his when, in fact, Thespis had assigned him to portray them. This was, in a word, historic.

THE HISTORY OF THE SYSTEM AND THE METHOD

In the early 1900s, Constantine Stanislavski, a Russian, formed a theater group called The Moscow Art Theatre. This group performed throughout Russia and then began to tour other countries. The theater group came to America for the first time in 1910, at which time Americans witnessed a theatrical revolution as marvelous and extreme as the Greeks had witnessed under the direction of Thespis nearly fourteen hundred years earlier.

Stanislavski is called the grandfather of modern acting. He is my grandfather, the grandfather of the teachers who taught me, and your grandfather. He was the first to dissect, revolutionize, and then systematize the art of acting. Stanislavski's System is his legacy to us.

Previous to Stanislavski's time, an actor portraying a particular emotion would make an exaggerated physical gesture to indicate that he was feeling the emotion. If he wanted to portray fear, for instance, he might raise his hands, widen his eyes, and drop his mouth open. But he was merely using his body to signify emotions he was not feeling. That style of acting is called *indicating*. It is an old, outgrown style that today makes us laugh. We call it "bad" acting because, thanks to Stanislavski, we've learned that it is devoid of the truthfulness that makes acting "good."

Stanislavski was the first to see that acting is good when "acting is living on stage." He maintained that the actor must feel the emotions he is representing. Stanislavski's System is, simply, his method of how to make the experience of acting real for the actor and, consequently, for the audience.

Compared to feeling the emotions themselves, Stanislavski put very little importance on the way the body responds as a result of those feelings; he believed that the emotions were primary—everything, in fact—and that the appropriate bodily gestures would naturally correspond. He and his fellow actors and actresses *lived* their roles on the stage. Using their experience and imagination, they actually felt the desire, fear, anger, love, lust, and ambition that their predecessors had first only sung about and then, later, merely pretended to feel, and the gestures of their bodies corresponded naturally.

And the people went nuts. They had never seen this kind of acting before—this raw, honest display of emotional truth—and it touched them deeply. It moved them in a way that was surprising and shattering. Sometimes terrified, sometimes thrilled, sometimes offended by their new theatrical experiences, people were jolted from convention and apathy by this new art, and they became recipients of greater emotional understanding.

When The Moscow Art Theatre again toured in New York in 1922, Lee Strasberg, a Jewish garment industry worker and women's hairpiece salesman, went to see them perform. He went again and again. So impressed was he by this new system or method of acting that electrified the stage that he began to study with the two teachers Stanislavski had assigned to remain and teach it in New York, Maria Ouspenskaya and Richard Boleslavsky, who later headed The American Laboratory Theatre.

Once Strasberg began to understand Stanislavski's System, he began to teach it to other actors in New York. He put his own little spin on the ball and called it Strasberg's Method. In 1930 he became partners with Harold Clurman, a director, and Cheryl Crawford, a producer. Together they founded The Group Theatre, where Strasberg taught his method.

Like The Moscow Art Theatre, The Group is another great legacy in theater. It included many fine actors, dancers, and singers, many of whom, like Strasberg, later became teachers of acting—spawning further offshoots and variations of Stanislavski's System. Among them were Stella Adler, Uta Hagan, Robert Lewis, and Sandy Meisner. Despite technical variations, as well as the controversies that grew out of some of them, Stanislavski's System has been and still is recognized by all who teach the American method of acting as its indisputable foundation.

One such technical disagreement and resulting controversy played a central role in breaking up The Group. It was over the value of a technique Strasberg termed "affective memory." During The Group's ten-year existence, from 1930 to 1940, Strasberg had thought that he and Stanislavski were in agreement on the definition, function, and value of affective memory. Then Stella Adler, a member of The Group, went to Paris to study privately with Stanislavski. She returned and informed Strasberg and The Group that Strasberg's evaluation of affective memory was wrong. The Group factionalized as a result of this controversy, and soon after disbanded in 1941.

THE STANISLAVSKI-STRASBERG CONTROVERSY

If you, the actor, need to come up with an emotion night after night and keep the experience real and fresh each time, you need a handy tool. Strasberg's most esteemed tool or technique for keeping the emotion real was *affective memory*. In affective memory, the actor recalls a personal experience that evokes the emotion needed for the performance. For example, let's say you need to express grief. You choose from your own past a powerful memory of grief and then, concentrating deeply, you employ *sense memory* to make the emotion come alive again in the present. Sense memory means remembering what you saw, heard, felt, tasted, and smelled during that time. Strasberg thought that reawakening all the actor's sense perceptions that were active during the time he or she felt a strong emotion was the most effective method for re-enlivening the emotion, thus making it "real" on stage.

When Stella Adler returned from studying with Stanislavski in Paris, however, she reported that Stanislavski did not agree with Strasberg on this point. On the contrary, according to Adler, Stanislavski believed that every memory, no matter how strong initially, has a fairly short psychic shelf life. He believed that imagination was a far better tool to use because imagination is always regenerating and exceeding itself with new ideas and, therefore, never goes stale or wears out.

History has further recorded that not only did Stella Adler return to The Group as the bearer of conflict and controversy, but that she broke the news bluntly and with no regrets. She and Strasberg had butted heads before. According to Adler, Stanislavski had said simply that Strasberg "was wrong," which had the effect of dividing The Group's members into factions and finally led to The Group breaking up.

For the record, Lorrie Hull, one of my teachers, was in Paris on the fiftieth anniversary of Stanislavski's death in 1988 and spoke with Stanislavski's granddaughter, Cyrilla Falk. Hull is the author of the best-selling book on acting, *Strasberg's Method*, and was Strasberg's senior faculty member at the Lee Strasberg Institute in Los Angeles for twelve years. During this meeting, Falk told Hull that at the end of his life Stanislavski said he agreed with Strasberg after all, that it was more important to use your experience than your imagination. Nonetheless, whether he did or did not say this, or did or did not agree with Strasberg, Stanislavski clearly stated in his writings that imagination gives the actor's feelings wings, while Strasberg held to his belief that if the actor used his imagination more than his experience, he wouldn't feel emotion deeply enough.

Uta Hagan, who was also a member of The Group and has been teaching since then, uses an approach that combines the two. She coaches the actor to invest his or her past emotion into a particular object during preparation and then to place that object, as a prop, on stage to cue the emotion he or she wishes to evoke. Let's say, using our earlier example, that you have to evoke grief for each performance. To do that, you elect to recall, from your past, the grief you felt when your father died. But let's also say that you are finding it difficult to reach repeatedly into that emotion through affective memory. For one thing, doing this can be quite time consuming. According to Adler, one of Stanislavski's objections to affective memory was that it is too demanding on the actor; the actor has to prepare for it so early in each performance so that he "has it" by the time he needs it. Hagan's solution is to take a particular (or similar) object that was in the room with you when your father died, such as a blue vase, and in your armchair preparation invest the memory and power of the grief in the vase, so that when you look at the vase, it elicits the grief you felt when your father died, and you cry because it reminds you of your loss. You then instruct the prop person to place the vase on stage so it is there to help you when you need it.

THE METHOD IS FOR THE ACTOR, NOT THE ACTOR FOR THE METHOD

Although every teacher has his or her own method or combination of methods, which he or she thinks is the best way to help you generate real emotions on stage, it ultimately comes down to you. You, the actor, must develop and use whatever method is best for you. Every teacher puts his or her own spin on the Stanislavski ball. But the method—*any* method—is made for the actor, the actor is not made for the method. Because no method has any value unless you find it to be valuable to *you*.

❁ *Affirmation*

I have my individual way. It is intelligently ordered and directed.

HOW TO SELECT YOUR NEXT TEACHER

I recommend that you have several acting teachers and coaches throughout your acting life. I also recommend that before you select your next one, you interview the teachers you are considering, audit their classes if permitted, and trust your instincts to lead you to the perfect next teacher for you.

I coach mostly privately now, but when I teach classes, I never allow auditing. I don't want anyone sitting in judgment over my students, each of whom gets up and works every class. There is no just sitting and observing in my classes. I do, however, allow a newcomer to take one class, during which I require that he or she also works. For private coaching, I invite prospective students to come and chat with me for half an hour or to book one session with me before they sign up for a month. For, while I am aware of my value to those with whom I am a good match, I recognize that not every teacher is for every student.

Remember that each of your acting teachers is there to serve you. It is *your* acting career. All of us who are good teachers know that. If you find a teacher who is a frustrated actor or actress who never made it and, consequently, comes at you with anger and resentment, bail. You don't need it. That's his or her problem. You need a teacher who will work for you, help you, teach you what he or she knows, and guide and encourage you. You do not need a teacher who yells at you or belittles you. You need one who knows what he or she is talking about *and* is able to transmit that information to you in a way that is clear and makes you feel understood, respected, and happy. Otherwise, dump 'em.

The point of the process here is to help you find *your* way to make the emotions and experiences happen on stage as real experiences. If it is real for you, it will be real for the audience. Look for teachers that help you achieve that. And when you've received—and paid handsomely for—what they had to offer you, thank them, bless them, and move on.

✖ EXERCISE

Write a brief paragraph describing what you think you already know about acting, as well as what you think you might gain from studying or training with the teacher or teachers you are considering hiring to help you.

_____

_____

_____

_____

_____

_____

SUMMARY OF MAIN POINTS

1. There are two main theories concerning the origin of theater: (1) it was a ritual to entertain and appease the gods and (2) it is an expression of our natural instinct to tell stories in an effort to better understand our own experiences and help others.
2. Theater has been with us always; it is a fundamental activity of a healthy society.
3. History dates the beginning of modern drama at 534 BC in Greece, when it was officially recognized as part of a religious festival during which a contest for the best tragedy was held. The winner of the contest, Thespis, directed an actor to speak the lines that Thespis wrote.
4. In the early 1900s, Constantine Stanislavski systematized acting as the art of actually living and feeling on stage the emotions the actor is assigned to represent. This revolutionized drama. Stanislavski called his approach Stanislavski's System.
5. In the 1920s, Lee Strasberg studied Stanislavski's System, put his own spin on the ball, began to teach it, and called it Strasberg's Method.
6. Every teacher since has put his or her own spin on the ball, but Stanislavski's System remains the foundation for most instructors who are teaching acting today.
7. Although it is invaluable to study the masters, every actor must find his or her own method of making the experience of acting on the stage emotionally authentic for him- or herself.

CHAPTER 10

No Shortcuts on
Learning Your Craft

*I don't find acting very easy. It's a lot of hard work
for me. But I love it. I love the homework, the research, and the solitude that goes into a part.*

—Bob Hoskins

No shortcuts? you ask. Well, let me ask you something: Why
should there be? You already have your tool kit filled with
your main tools of experience and imagination and everything
else you need. Why should there be a shortcut in learning how
to act? How about just letting it take the time that it takes?

We are afflicted in our culture with "get rich quick" dis-
ease. We're on the lookout to make a quick killing. We believe
that if we could just get to know the right somebody, we could
beat the system and get in. It's who you know, we're told, not
who you are or what you have to offer. This all comes from
the mistaken belief that being successful results from some kind
of trick or magic. If we just knew the magic formula, we could
transform our lives of hum-drum mediocrity into a brilliant,

dazzling existence, allowing us to by-pass everything—especially work—on our way up to the pinnacle of success.

It would be great if it worked that way, wouldn't it? I'd be the first one to line up for it. But, unfortunately, it doesn't. And all the time that we spend trying to find shortcuts only takes time away from getting down to doing what *does* get the job done. Don't try to learn your craft of acting too quickly. Don't skip some of the work, memorize too soon, or try to rush to the top. Life is a process. It's a journey—not a destination. And "success" is an ongoing process.

I recently saw Carol Burnett being interviewed by James Lipton on the Bravo series "Inside the Actors' Studio." Lipton asked her, "When did you feel that you had finally made it?" Carol looked at him surprised and said, "I have never felt that I've made it. I don't feel that I *have* made it." Now this is Carol Burnett, one of the most successful women in show business. "Once you feel that you've made it," she added, "it's over."

That's one of life's wonderful keys, one of the joys that keeps us going—the realization that there's always more we can achieve. If you occupy yourself with hunting for get-rich-quick schemes and shortcuts, you rob yourself of enjoying the work process. You certainly, at least, postpone it. And you waste your precious time.

To truly succeed, you must love the entire process and be thorough in your work of acting, because the delight comes from doing the work. And the sooner you submit to this process, the sooner you will succeed. You have a huge task ahead of you each time you take on a role: you are about to elucidate truth for an audience. Realize that. Realize that the merchandise of your trade consists of imbibing and expressing ideas of love, truth, and beauty. You are enlightening minds, comforting hearts, and freeing souls. Be willing to do this fully and thoroughly and to stay with it until it is done.

There are three stories that I hope will give you more

insight into the value of approaching your acting work with the understanding of its magnificence and, thus, with reverence.

THE DEVOTEE AND THE MONK

A struggling devotee had traveled a long way to see a great monk before whom he knelt down and prayed, "Please, holy father, teach me to be a great monk like you are."

The monk answered with a light, compassionate laugh, "You're not ready, my son," and he started to walk away.

But the young devotee would not be discouraged. "Please, father, I am strong," he said, although he was very tired. "I can do anything. Just give me the chance to prove myself to you."

The great monk studied him for a moment. Touched by his sincerity, he yielded. Nodding toward a long white fence in front of which he was standing, he said, "Paint the fence green." And then he walked away.

The devotee was delighted. This would be a piece of cake, he thought. He rose, found some paint, and soon he had painted the fence green. Afterward he stood back and looked at his work. He was proud of himself. He had done the work well and had exercised diligence and patience while doing so. He closed the last can of paint with a tap, cleaned his brush, and set out to find the great monk, certain that the monk would now agree to take him under his tutelage.

"I painted the fence green, father," he said proudly when he was once again kneeling before the monk. "And I believe I did a very good job of it. Now, will you teach me to be a monk?"

With a nearly imperceptible gleam in his eye, the monk replied, "I'm sorry, my son, but you are not ready to be a monk."

The devotee was dashed. He wanted to cry out, "Why not? I did what you told me!" but he held his tongue. "What more must I do?" he asked.

"Go back and paint the fence white," replied the monk.

The devotee was annoyed. He wanted to say, "If you wanted it white, why did you tell me to paint it green?!" But again he held his tongue. In a moment it began to dawn on him that the great monk was testing him. He resolved to pass the test.

Dismissing his anger and humbling his will, he proceeded to paint the fence white. Using the same qualities of diligence and patience that had grown by his previous exercise of them—which was fortunate because this time he had to give the fence two coats to cover the green—he painted the fence white. He was certain that this time the monk would agree to teach him to be a great monk.

"Father, I have completed my task," he said when he'd found him. "I've painted the fence white. Now will you teach me to be a monk?"

But the monk said, "I'm sorry, my son. You're not ready to be a monk. Paint the fence green."

This time the devotee was too annoyed to even try to mask his anger. He was exhausted and now began to suspect that he was being made sport of. And yet, as he watched the monk walk away from him again, he was once again struck by the notion that there was some method to the monk's direction. He rose from his knees and returned to the fence.

Chanting softly to keep himself calm—and awake—he set back to work. This time, though, he became more absorbed in the process. He actually enjoyed the work of painting the fence green. When he had finished, he stepped back and looked at his work. "This is a beautifully painted green fence," he thought, feeling less pride and more satisfaction this time. He cleaned his brush and set out again to find the monk.

"Father," he said, "I have once again painted the fence green. Will you now teach me to be a monk?" He was certain that this time his request would be granted, especially since he'd learned to take more satisfaction from the moment.

But for the fourth time, the monk refused. "You are not ready, my son," he said. "Go back and paint the fence white."

Angry, disappointed, and nearly catatonic with disbelief and exhaustion, the devotee sat back on his heels in the dirt for a few minutes and then returned to the fence and painted it white.

The fifth time he came before the monk he didn't even bother to ask for what he wanted. He saw refusal in the monk's eye and knew what he next had to do. Without even grumbling, he simply returned to the fence and painted the damn thing green.

Once again, he returned to the monk. Before even asking, he perceived that his desire was denied. Once again, he returned and repainted the long fence white.

Finally, thoroughly exhausted in body, mind, and will, the young man came back to the monk and stood before him. He did not kneel, he did not ask, he did not even want anything any more.

The great monk smiled at him. "What is your wish, my son?" he asked him.

"My wish, father," said the devotee, "is simply to do your will. I will go back and paint the fence green."

As he turned to leave, the monk stopped him. "There is no need to paint the fence green," he said with a twinkle in his eye. "The fence is perfectly fine painted white. There was never a need to do anything *to the fence.*"

At first the devotee was stunned. But then the meaning of the great monk's teaching dawned on him. He had been taught that greatness is achieved by humble submission to an ongoing *process*, as opposed to the worldly modus operandi of blindly striking out to achieve a *goal*. Now it was he who smiled, gratefully, at the great monk who, in fact, the very moment the devotee had first asked him, had taken him under his tutelage.

The point here is that the human ego would rush around and get its pencils sharpened and paper in order and say, "OK,

I'm ready to be taught." But the marvelous paradox is that before it becomes teachable, the will must humble itself by surrendering to the teaching process. Then it will find that it already knows everything it wishes to know.

THE SAMURAI AND THE MONK

Once there was a very great samurai. A great and mighty warrior, he was feared throughout the land. He had killed many enemies and had many victories to his credit. People quaked when they heard that the samurai was coming. They did everything in their power to please him to assuage his wrath.

But the samurai, while he appreciated his own achievements and enjoyed the respect and praise he received from others, felt that there was something missing in his life. He had tamed the earth—nothing outside him could overpower him—but he had not attained peace in his thinking. So he set off on a pilgrimage to learn to do so.

One day, he came to a humble monk and fell down respectfully before him. "Holy father," he said, "please teach me about heaven and hell."

The little monk said, "*You?!* You've got to be kidding me! You, a horrible, smelly, disgusting, sinning samurai, want me to teach you of heaven and hell? You are so ignorant and gross and stupid that you would never be able to learn about such important matters. You are a waste of life. You probably aren't even a very good samurai. You probably even have a dull blade on your sword!"

The samurai was enraged. Smoke was coming out of his ears and nose, and his eyes were popping out of their sockets. He unsheathed his shiny (and very sharp) sword and, with a primal scream erupting from his very bowels, lifted it over his head and was about to slice the little monk into two equally sized portions when the monk looked deeply into the samurai's insane stare and said softly, "*That* is hell."

Blown completely away, the samurai dropped his sword and fell on his face at the feet of the monk. "Oh, my father," he cried humbly, "forgive me! I am unworthy to receive your great teaching. Forgive my pride and my ignorance, holy father."

The monk knelt down beside the abject samurai and, when the samurai raised his tear-filled eyes to look at him, said tenderly, "And *that*, my son, is heaven."

❈ Affirmation

I can do all things through God, which strengthens me.

READING A PART TEN TIMES

As with the devotee and the samurai who had to become humble before they were able to learn the deeper values to which they aspired, there is something very beautiful and necessary to the Zen idea of reading a part ten times before you ever have the audacity to think that you are ready to begin to work on it. Why is that so? Because in acting you are undertaking a truly grand work.

You will experience a wonderful phenomenon if you exercise the humility and discipline to first read your part ten times. Sure, you know you've absorbed everything that's in there by the time you've read it three times. It's not rocket science here. And you're not an idiot, right? It's about what it's about and you get it and that's that! But by the sixth or seventh, or eighth time you've read it, things will start showing up that you never would have seen if you had started memorizing those lines before fully understanding them. "Oh, my God," we think, "I've got to memorize those lines!" and hurry up and get out on stage to start being adored. But that's not what acting is about. Acting is deciphering and understanding the state of mind you are to represent and then finding your way to embody, imbibe, and *be* it, time and again on stage or in front of the camera for the purpose of honoring truth and benefiting your audience. And to the degree that you do the work methodically, slowing your pace down to whatever speed will best ensure that you do that, you will decrease your anxiety, do a good job, and increase your enjoyment of the process and confidence that you *know* that you know what you are doing.

KNOWING THAT YOU KNOW

It's one thing to know something, isn't it? But *to know* that you know it is even sweeter. It is tremendously empowering. It gives you confidence. And you only get that feeling when you realize that it is the whole process that is acting, not just the activity on stage, and commit to doing your preparation work thoroughly. You won't lessen your passion or your inspiration by being thoroughly prepared any more than learning to read music and practicing lessens a musician's natural, instinctual ability. On the contrary, it frees, emboldens, and furthers it. So embrace the whole process. Learn what the experts say, and then do it your way.

EXERCISE

Please complete the following sentences:

1. It's not the work that stops me from following my dreams, it is ______________________________

______________________________.

2. Before I can actually get down to taking my acting seriously and staying with it until it bears fruit, ____________

____

______________________________.

NAAMAN, THE LEPER

Naaman was a great warrior from Damascus. In spite of his military prowess and achievements, he was also a leper, a victim of a terrible physical affliction for which there was no known medical cure. He had heard of an Israelite monk named Elisha who could cure leprosy, so he made a pilgrimage to Israel to find and petition Elisha to heal him.

When Naaman met the simple, unworldly Elisha, he went out of his way to greet Elisha with a degree of respect far beyond what Naaman felt was socially due him. He thereby expected special treatment from Elisha. But Elisha simply told Naaman to dip himself in the Israelites' River Jordan to be healed.

Naaman was a great man but he was also possessed of great pride. He took offense and rode away in a rage.

"The River Jordan, indeed! Are not Abana and Pharpar, rivers of Damascus, better than all the waters of Israel?" he demanded of his servants, who were traveling with him. "May I not wash in them and be clean?"

His servants answered, "Father, if you had been asked to do some great thing, would you not have done it?"

Naaman got it. He understood that he was being asked not to be great—which was easy for him—but to be modest. Being asked to do a small thing offended him because he had become used to doing only great things in his own way that few others could do. And he had assessed his self-worth and power accordingly.

That power had not been great enough to cure him of leprosy, however; he now saw that pride had been keeping him from experiencing true power. Humbled, he did as Elisha had prescribed—his very action proving that he had been cleansed of his pride. He went back to Elisha, healed.

How important it is to do those small things, those line-by-line readings, those little by little everyday practices of preparation. By the end of the week, the month, the year, you will have developed a firm base and grown to a respectable height from which you will never topple. Stanislavski said, "The great majority of actors are convinced that they need to work only at rehearsals and that at home they can enjoy their leisure. But this is not so. In rehearsals an actor merely clarifies the work he should be doing at home." Goethe agreed. "An actor's career develops in public," he said, "but his art develops only in private."

DO IT ALL

Here are some things you can do:

1. Read the masters. Read the writings of Constantine Stanislavski, Lee Strasberg, Uta Hagan, Sanford Meisner, Robert Lewis, Michael Checkhov, Michael Shurtleff, S. Loraine Hull, and whoever else strikes your fancy. Hang out at Samuel French Bookstore, Drama Book Shop, or other bookstores in your neighborhood that cater to the theater. Go to the library and take books out; you don't have to buy them. Find the ones that really work for you; buy those.

2. Study with several teachers. Get everyone's take on this thing called "acting," then formulate your own.

3. Talk and work with other actors. Find out how they think, how they work, who they study with, how they prepare. Get *down* with all this! Make it your priority. Be philosophical, experimental, intellectual, and creative.

4. Find out what productions are going on in your area in colleges and community theaters and on local television. Try to get involved.

5. Visit college film departments and see if you can become part of the crews working on graduate films, and then work yourself into one of the film's smaller roles. Don't feel like you're too good for things, too good to start small. (Remember Naaman and his pride.) A lot of people make this mistake and it keeps them from making their first efforts, which consequently postpones their success. We'd all like to start at the top, but if you try to do that, it might take years to begin at all. And when you finally do, you will have to start at the beginning, anyway. So you might as well do it now.

6. Look into extra casting and do some extra work.

7. Do your spiritual work daily. This is your most important daily practice; it opens your vision and helps you recognize the opportunities that do come your way—which are always around you but which, until you are open, you don't see.

8. Be adventurous; think about putting on a play or making a short film. We love leaders who give us opportunities that would otherwise never have come our way; be one of those leaders.

The point is: Commit. Commit to acting as your art, your business, and your calling; then follow the inspiration that will come from making that commitment. Then stay with it!

❊ EXERCISE

List three things that you agree to do for your acting career this week. Think about it first, because you are making a commitment.

1. _____

_____

2. _____

_____

3. ____

____

Now schedule them, and make sure that you do them. If there are any commitments or promises that you should definitely keep, they are the ones that you make to yourself!

Yes, acting is a collaborative business. You may not be able to star in a multimillion-dollar production right away unless your mother owns the controlling interest in General Motors, but there are many things that you *can* do. If you want to act, you will have to train and apprentice yourself. You must put yourself through your own self-designed program. But everything that you need is at your disposal. That's the good news. And the commitment to begin, the humility to begin at the beginning, and the willingness to give all that it takes will ensure your success.

EXERCISE

Be ten years old again and answer the following question, What do you want to be when you grow up?

____

SUMMARY OF MAIN POINTS

1. In our culture we are besieged with get-rich-quick schemes. Not only do they not work, these so-called shortcuts rob us of much time before we finally give them up and get down to work.
2. Life is a process, a journey—not a destination.
3. Love being thorough in your work, for the delight is in the work itself. Don't try to hurry it. Work on a solid basis and you will reap the greatest satisfaction.
4. Recognize and honor the importance of your work as an actor. You are enlightening minds, comforting hearts, and freeing souls.

CHAPTER 11

Discovering Your Niche in the Play

I have no preference about the parts I play. I prefer neither saints nor sinners. I can only create characters in which I believe.

—Paul Scofield

Your part "in the play" has two interrelated aspects. The first is your part in the cosmic play, life itself, which is to be the living expression of all that is magnificent in life. The way you do that within society—your job—is to be an actor. That is the means by which you express your highest ideals in the world. The second aspect is your part or niche within the dramas or plays themselves.

Plays are collaborations. It takes a lot of money to put on a play, and a great deal more to put on a television show or produce a film. So, unless you have enough money to finance your own acting career in which you can star in any drama you choose, then you would do well to find your own particular path of least resistance—the Tao of your acting career, the roles where you will most likely be recognized as the perfect actor to play them. In other words, play the "really challenging roles" that are, in fact, least suited to you on your own time, for fun and for growth. But if you want to have acting as a career, then find your particular niche in the play—the roles that you can play most effectively. This won't limit you. It will give you an intelligent way to get your foot in the door in keeping with who you are and what you have to offer. So I'm all for typecasting—at the beginning. Once you have a foothold, you can broaden your scope if you like.

For instance, I am a five-foot-six woman who weighs 125 pounds and has blonde hair and blue eyes. Therefore, I am not likely to be cast to play the part of a big, buff, black man. That doesn't adversely limit me, however, or keep me from having any fun in life. What it does do is help match me up with certain roles for which I will more likely be cast. It guides me toward something that has a higher probability of happening. If I keep going out, or my agent keeps sending me out, for the parts of big, muscular black men and I keep getting turned down (and probably ridiculed), not only is this not going to do anything to further my career, it's going to damage my self-esteem. And to what end? A dead end! I am going to be cast, first of all, in the role of a woman. From there I can define it even further to certain states of mind that would be the most natural for me to play, the avenues through which, most easily and with least resistance and stretch of the imagination, I can contribute. And what's wrong with that? What is the sense in making it harder for yourself or the director or the audience? Believe me, every role is a challenge. Acting is a hard job. But it is also a privilege. And no one is out there just waiting to finance the whims of some actor who doesn't know what he can do and wants to play Hamlet when he should be playing Macbeth.

KNOW YOUR PRODUCT

Which brings us to an important point. You, the actor, are your own product. You and your take on things is what you have to offer. You must, therefore, know what that is. Any salesperson will tell you that you are only going to make a fool of yourself if you go on a sales call without a clear idea about what your product can do and what your customer wants. If you bring in an orange slicer, say, but your customer is really looking for an eggbeater—you are not going to make the sale. And if you try to convince him that your orange slicer can also be an eggbeater if just given half a chance—which is what actors do all the time—you are only going to convince your customer that you are both unknowledgeable and loopy. If you stubbornly promote yourself for an unsuitable part, you will only succeed in convincing the director that you are insensitive to the play and his needs to cast the part properly. And that director won't want to do business with you in the future.

Know what you, as your product, can do best. And, I'm sorry—because I know this might hurt—but you can't do everything. Take a break and grieve over that fact for a minute, if you need to, but it's true. And the sooner you realize it, the sooner you will see that it's really OK. You don't have to do everything. We've got other people to do the other things. We need *you* to be *you* and do what *you* do. Cool, huh? I mean, when you think about it, that's good planning and a relief. So just figure out what *you* can do—most naturally, most easily, most effortlessly—and do that. And make that discovery *now*. Only by determining and then working on the roles that you believe you are most suited to play will you gain some control over what you do play.

When you are clear what your castability is—which I will help you determine in chapter 12—then the directors and producers who are in the position of hiring you will also see your vision, because it is accurate, and you will be hired. Maybe not all the time, but often enough to give you a lucrative and satisfying career.

◉ *Affirmation*

I am caused by my source to be in my right place and to flourish.

THE RIGHT FIT

You can trust your vision when you are being honest with yourself. And you will start working as an actor much more quickly and regularly as a result of your honest inner market research. Then, once your foot is in the door, you can branch out and do other roles if you like. But I will bet that even after you've become a star, 90 percent of the time you will choose to continue to do the same kinds of parts as a result of this soul (and *role*) searching. Because I'm not asking you to pick parts that *don't* fit you, but those that do. And I'm trusting that if you think they fit you, they will be the kinds of roles that you'll also want to do.

We're talking about the Tao of acting here as well as the Tao of casting—two intersecting paths of least resistance. And it starts with you: Know where you readily fit and can best serve the play and be willing to serve it in that way. The result? You will work more often and have more opportunities to get better at your craft.

✳ EXERCISE

This exercise is great for concentration, improvisation, trusting in yourself, self-confidence, and timing. Clap your hands and stamp your foot in unison, at the rate of two claps per second. Once you have established a steady rhythm, begin to recite the alphabet. State the letter, and then follow with a quality that you possess that begins with that letter, such as A, altruistic; B, beautiful; C, classy; D, dangerous; E, eloquent. Speak on every beat. Let the qualities come off the top of your head; improvise, but mean it. If you can't think of something, repeat the letter until you do (F, F, F, fabulous). Do it until you are able to go through the entire alphabet without a glitch.

And remember, every adjective you have claimed about yourself in this exercise, is true about you!

SUMMARY OF MAIN POINTS

1. It is wise to take the paths of least resistance in life; they mark your way. So, too, in acting. Discover the Tao of your acting career—the roles in which you most naturally and effortlessly fit and most effectively contribute to the play, the audience, and the world.

2. You, the actor, are your own product. You must know what your product can do. It can't do everything, but that's OK. We've got other people to do other things. We've got you to be you.

3. Define who you, as an actor, are, and then start working and getting sharp on those kinds of roles. You will then be able to transmit your vision to your agent as well as to the directors and producers who audition you, and you will be hired more often than if you remain a nonspecific generality.

4. Rather than limiting you, this approach helps you to get your foot in the door more quickly and inside a place that is satisfying to you. Later you can branch out and do other types of roles if you want to, but by working this way, you will have found your niche.

CHAPTER 12

Castability Profiling

Let every actor achieve outer characterization by using material from his own life and that of others, real or imaginary. But in all this external search, an actor must never lose his own identity.

—Constantine Stanislavski

In this chapter I will help you analyze who you are as an actor through what I have termed "castability profiling." The various exercises will give you insight and guidance about the roles you are best suited for. By chapter's end you'll have a clear sense of what you have to offer. Then I'll help you write up a sales pitch that will effectively present your vision of yourself as an actor to a prospective agent.

But first let me explain how castability profiling works in my seminars and workshops.

FEAR AND LOVE

In the castability profiling portion of my seminars and workshops, I ask each member of the workshop to come to the front of the room and sit in a chair facing the rest of the group. I begin by asking the actor in the hot seat two questions. The first question is, "What scares you the most about acting?" The second is, "What appeals to you the most about acting?" I ask the actor to spend one full minute answering each question. The answers provide the other members of the workshop a quick glimpse into the personality and mind-set—beyond the obvious physicality—of the actor in front of them. This information prepares them for the second part of the exercise in which they profile the actor—offer their perceptions and opinions as to the type of actor he or she is and what roles best suit him or her.

In our case, since you and I will be working alone, this entire exercise will be more introspective. Answering those questions will prime the pump for the work you will do later when *you* determine for yourself what roles you are best suited for. I believe you will find your answers to these questions stimulating.

Without trying to preformulate an answer, please write down, off the top of your head, your answers. There are no right or wrong answers, except insofar as you have answered honestly or not. Don't judge yourself; just let it rip. See if you can unearth what you really feel.

What scares you the most about acting?

_____

_____

What appeals to you the most about acting?

_____

_____

You now have the benefit of seeing in black and white what your thoughts on the subject are. Just for the heck of it, would you like to know what, in my twelve years of teaching, I have found to be the five most common answers to each of the two questions?

What scares you the most about acting?
1. That I won't be able to do it. I'll look incompetent or I'll go overboard and look like an idiot.
2. The uncertainty of it all. Those waiting and not-knowing periods of "did I get the part or not?" Dealing with the constant fear that I might not make it.
3. The business aspect of acting—the people, the harshness, the temptations and possible corruption, the loss of anonymity that comes with success.
4. Mediocrity—that I'll just get by but never be able to go deep enough to become really good at acting.
5. Stage fright; freezing up and forgetting my lines on stage.

What appeals to you the most about acting?
1. The feeling that I'm following my heart and doing what I want to do, plus being part of a creative endeavor with other interesting people.
2. The psychological aspect of being other people by which I bring out something in myself I otherwise wouldn't, including being able to act out my aggressions and dreams.
3. The excitement of feeling fully present in the moment and completely spontaneous with something I rehearsed over and over.
4. The attention, appreciation, praise, glamour, and money—plus the endless opportunities all that gives you.
5. The partnership with an audience—touching and inspiring them, making a difference in their lives.

Interesting, isn't it? It's always interesting to see how other people think and how our thinking compares with theirs. But nothing is more interesting than knowing what we think ourselves. Now do one more thing: Compare your answers to the common answers and make an analytical comment.

_____
_____
_____

Notice, if you will, that I asked you what scared you the most before I asked you what appealed to you the most. There was a reason for that. I believe we need to get our fears out—exposed, recognized, disarmed, and then dismissed. And there is nothing that disarms and dismisses fear more effectively than love. So, when you are able to expose the fear, get it out of hiding, and then keep it to the side as you then take a look at what you love about something, you will find that, to a significant degree, your love will have outshone, overcome, displaced, and destroyed the fear, without much effort on your part. Isn't that what is happening to you right now? Aren't you now less afraid of acting than you were before you exposed your fear and then took a stand for what you loved about it? Take heart. It is your love of acting that will destroy everything that will resist and oppose it.

PUBLIC CASTABILITY PROFILING

Once the actor on the hot seat has spoken extemporaneously for two minutes or so, I give him or her a pad of paper and a pencil and instruct him or her to take notes. I tell the actor to keep his or her eyes on the paper and refrain from commenting, either with gestures, facial expressions, or words, on what he or she is about to hear. The actor is simply to gather information and write it down, which will only come freely if the group members feel completely uncensored. Once this agreement is made, I ask the other members of the group, whom the actor sits facing, two questions.

The first is: "What actors working today does this actor remind us of?" The names come fast and furious as members of the group shout them out. Some are very surprising. Some are amusing. Some are even perceived by the actor as insulting. But most of them carry a collective agreement from the group as a whole, and the actor simply scurries to write them all down.

After this has gone on for a few minutes, I ask the second question: "If it were up to us to cast this actor, in what types of roles would we cast him or her? What do we see him or her most easily playing?" Before I allow them to answer this question, however, I again remind the actor, "No comments from the peanut gallery, please. Just write it all down." This is strictly an information-gathering process, the content of which the actor may later analyze and accept or dismiss on his or her own. The members of the group are objective; they don't know the actor and have no emotional investment in the observations they are making. They neither resent nor are jealous of the actor, nor support the actor beyond everyday brotherly kindness. And I don't want reactions from the actor to taint that objectivity.

Again, the comments come fast and furious: "I see her playing a truck-stop waitress, a re-hab counselor, a lawyer, a rock-and-roll star, a working mom." "I see him playing a priest, a basketball player, an addict."

Each person in the group gets his or her turn on the hot seat to see how he or she is perceived by others. It's always a confidence boost because the actor realizes that he or she is perceived by others as similar and comparable to currently successful actors, as well as believably castable in a variety of roles. The information may be surprising, but it is generally supportive and always very interesting for everyone involved.

PRIVATE CASTABILITY PROFILING: THE ORANGE SHEET

But what if you are not in a group? That's why I created the Orange Sheet. I call it the Orange Sheet because one day I had it copied on orange paper, and it's been the Orange Sheet ever since.

The Orange Sheet is the method I have devised to uncover and provide to the individual the castability information one may get from attending one of my workshops. I am providing it for you here the same way that I provide it for my private student clients with whom I work one on one, and if you will follow my instructions, you will reap the same benefits they do. Give yourself two hours to fill out the Orange Sheet so that you can really think through your answers. You need this time to bring up important answers from your psyche about your abilities and special acting niches.

The Orange Sheet consists of five sections. Sections 1 and 2 get you rolling, the heart of the exercise consists of Sections 3 and 4, and the soul is Section 5—by which you analyze all the information gathered in Sections 1 through 4. All sections are important for successfully completing the effort, which I believe you will find quite exciting.

❂ *Affirmation*

I am valuable, attractive, desired, needed, and appreciated. Tangibly!

All right, let's begin.

Section 1

List ten actors of the opposite sex whom you like, and something you like about his or her acting. *Example (if you are a man): Meryl Streep. She feels her emotions deeply and commits intensely to her choices. Example (if you are a woman): Cary Grant. He blends the sensibilities of the working-class man with those of the aristocrat with dignity and humor.* Whoever and whatever your choices are, as long as they are true, they are valid. The point is for you to be honest with yourself and to express yourself as clearly as possible.

1._____   _____
_____
2._____   _____
_____
3._____   _____

4. _____ _____

5. _____ _____

6. _____ _____

7. _____ _____

8. _____ _____

9. _____ _____

10. _____ _____

Good! Now that you have listed ten actors of the opposite gender, which got you rolling with the least amount of self-consciousness and sense of personal investment, you are now ready for Section 2.

Section 2

List ten actors of the same sex as you whom you like, and something you like about his or her acting. Don't worry about picking the "right" answers; just list who you like. Let it come up from your psyche without censorship or judgment. If you like Lassie, write down Lassie. As an artist, you've got to be willing to be a little bit of a dork because all of us are. And when you sign up to be an artist, you give up your right to hide.

1. _____ _____

2. _____ _____

3. _____ _____

4. _____ _____
   _____
5. _____ _____
   _____
6. _____ _____
   _____
7. _____ _____
   _____
8. _____ _____
   _____
9. _____ _____
   _____
10. _____ _____
    _____

Section 3

This section is the one most like the castability profiling that I conduct in my workshops. It has two parts.

1. Assume that you are presently a star, taking the lead roles, making the big bucks. List ten other stars working today whom you believe a producer or director would consider, along with you, for the same role.
2. List three roles each of these star actors have played.

To make this exercise work, you have to assume that you are, *now*, a star. In the castability profiling in my workshops, fellow workshop members do the work of identifying comparable actors according to *their* perceptions and opinions. Here, I'm asking *you* to identify which actors *you* believe you're similar to, which is, ultimately, more valuable, though perhaps not quite so ego gratifying.

Using myself as an example, let's say that Barbra Streisand or Jonathan Demme is considering me to star in her or his next film. I believe that, along with me, she or he would also be considering Goldie Hawn, Meryl Streep, Jessica Lange, and so on.

I list my ten according to what I think. Then, for the second part, I list three roles I've seen each of my choices play. For example: I've seen Goldie Hawn play a spoiled bitch who learns love is more important than money (*Overboard*); a fantasy-driven waitress who finds that, through love, her fantasies can come true (*The Housesitter*); and an aging self-centered actress who finally wakes up to what is valuable and puts her life on a steady footing (*First Wives' Club*). I do this for each of my ten.

Ready to do your ten? OK, here goes:

1._____

    a. _____

    b. _____

    c._____

2._____

    a. _____

    b. _____

    c._____

3._____

    a. _____

    b. _____

    c._____

4._____

    a. _____

    b. _____

    c._____

5._____

    a. _____

    b. _____

    c._____

6._____
   a. _____
   b. _____
   c._____

7._____
   a. _____
   b. _____
   c._____

8._____
   a. _____
   b. _____
   c._____

9._____
   a. _____
   b. _____
   c._____

10._____
   a. _____
   b. _____
   c._____

Section 4

List ten roles you feel you could comfortably play, plus their main action. Ask yourself what roles in society would you like to play, and think you could. What would the character be doing? And what would happen to the character? The choices are yours. Using myself, I might say that I could play a widow with teenage children who has a small horse farm in Kansas who comes up against financial difficulties, struggles, loses her ranch, but learns something important about herself and her family. It's up to me: I get to play the queen, a ruthless ball buster, a nun, *and* a junked-out prostitute.

Ready to list your ten? Here goes:

1. The role: _____
   Doing what: _____

   _____

   What happens: _____

   _____

2. The role: _____
   Doing what: _____

   _____

   What happens: _____

   _____

3. The role: _____
   Doing what: _____

   _____

   What happens: _____

   _____

4. The role: _____
   Doing what: _____

   _____

   What happens: _____

   _____

5. The role: _____
   Doing what: _____

   _____

   What happens: _____

   _____

6. The role: _____
   Doing what: _____

   _____

What happens: _____

_____

7. The role: _____
Doing what: _____

What happens: _____

_____

8. The role: _____
Doing what: _____

What happens: _____

_____

9. The role: _____
Doing what: _____

What happens: _____

_____

10. The role: _____
Doing what: _____

What happens: _____

_____

OK, here's a surprise for you. A cool offshoot of Section 4 is that you have just written the log lines for ten different stage or screenplays that *you* know *you are perfectly suited to star in!* Because these are roles that would be natural for you to play. This is who you are as an actor. You're so much more, as well, but here is a concrete start.

Section 5

Now analyze the previous four sections for common elements and insights into your current, most probable castability. Remember, acting is a business, and you are your product. So it certainly won't hurt you to see where you think you are best suited and, therefore, most likely to be cast at this time. Then, once you've gotten your foot in the door, you can break all your *own* rules.

ANALYZING YOUR ORANGE SHEET

You will notice when you begin to analyze the information on your Orange Sheet that there is commonality in various areas. You might find that three of the women that you admire, for instance, plus four of the women you think you might be considered along with for a role, usually play strong characters that deal with adversity but finally win. Or, you might find that five or six of the actors you like, as well as some of the roles that you think you could comfortably play, include the common elements of vulnerability, commitment, and intensity. Make note of these insights.

Another thing you might do is check the common qualities you liked about "the girls" and those you liked about "the boys"; then, too, how they differ from one another. Draw some parallels, make some distinctions, come to some conclusions, or just become aware of the information and let it float in your mind for a while. If you do this exercise thoroughly, you will be able to walk away from it with a good, practical sense of— and this is the key—what *you* believe is your current most probable and most satisfying castability. And I believe that you will be right. And all those abilities you admire in the actors and actresses in Sections 1 and 2? Those are abilities you have and yearn to develop and express, in yourself.

I believe that intelligence is omniscient and on the deepest level you know who you are and where you fit. It is your job as a marketing person to research your product—yourself—so that you become clear about what you've got in your sample case and then present that accurately when you go in to make a sale. You have to see it and believe it. Then you can sell it to an agent, then to a casting director, and then to a producer and director. But you've got to know. You can't be just sort of hoping that you're going to get some sort of role. You've got to know you are right for a particular role; otherwise you will not project the degree of authentic self-assurance necessary to inspire your prospective employers with enough confidence to hire you.

Once you get a sense of where you easily fit in, narrow it down further. I'm being ruthless here, I know, but this is business. Narrow it down to three or four types and roles. Then go in to your prospective new agent and say something like this:

> I'm most comfortable playing women with an ethical backbone who have some vulnerability—and a sense of humor—and come up against life's challenges and overcome them.
>
> Such as a sculptor, say, who falls in love and struggles to remain open and giving while, at the same time, staying true to herself. Or a businesswoman who fights for the underdog against the "big boys" and wins. Or a woman in the healing arts who is caught between the pressure of the establishment and her own view about what's best for her patient and fights for what she believes.
>
> Roles á la Susan Sarandon, or Meryl Streep, or a young Joanne Woodward—smart, caring, funny, down to earth. That's who I am. That's where I fit. That's where I think I can do the best job.

THE ACTOR'S SALES PITCH

I just slipped the above sales pitch in there as it came off the top of my head. It sounded natural and effortless, didn't it? Now I can tell you: that is the gist of the Orange Sheet; that's the real purpose of it—to get you to the point where you can deliver a short sales pitch or mission statement in your prospective new agent's office as if it is just coming off the top of your head. So let's break it down.

The text of the actor's sales pitch—garnered from the information on your Orange Sheet and your analysis of it—breaks down into three short paragraphs.

Paragraph 1: Make a general statement of the overall type of person in society today that you would feel the most natural and comfortable playing.

Paragraph 2: List three examples, which you can select from Section 4 of your Orange Sheet, of that type of person—his or her occupations, what he or she is up against, and how the story turns out. Choose three you feel, combined, pretty much cover your artistic ground. Remember, this is a sales pitch here, not an essay: You've got to make some choices. Be concise!

Paragraph 3: Give three examples of well-known actors who you feel you are like in type and temperament and who also play these kinds of roles. Doing this will help your prospects relate. You can pull these names from Section 3 of your Orange Sheet. Then, in a short sentence using three or four adjectives—which you can pull from Sections 1 and 2—sum up the common characteristics you and those three other actors have in common. Then say that is your story; who you, as an actor, are.

After you've written, memorized, and delivered your pitch in your interview, be quiet. Do not say, "Do you think I'm a nut, or egocentric, for comparing myself to stars; or joking?!" Just be quiet and listen. Listen for corroboration from your prospective agent that he or she sees you the way you do, as well as for his or her admiration and appreciation for your having articulated your vision so clearly. If, on the other hand, he or she doesn't see you that way at all, then hear that and say "thanks for your time" and split. But, I promise you, if you've been honest with yourself on your Orange Sheet, the former is more likely to happen. You will go in to your prospective agents and other representatives and say this is where you feel that you fit, these are the kinds of roles that you feel you can score and best play, and they will see your vision and buy it because you will be right about who you are, and you will have successfully transferred your vision to them. This, in turn, will inspire them with a sense of how to market you, which is their function in your life.

❋ EXERCISE

Make a two-hour appointment with yourself right now to fill out your Orange Sheet, then keep that appointment! Write your own twenty-second sales pitch that encapsulates who you, as an actor, are.

Remember, this is just your current castability that you are discovering through this process; it could change in a year. You can certainly check that in a year by once again doing the Orange Sheet; it's important to have an articulate sense of where you really think you are at every given moment. Find out where you are right now, then let the confidence that comes from that clarity support you as you hone your craft and begin to market the magnificent and needed product that you are.

SUMMARY OF MAIN POINTS

1. The purpose of the Orange Sheet is to bring up from your psyche or subconscious mind what you believe your abilities and niches in acting are.

2. If you follow the instructions on the Orange Sheet and do the exercises thoroughly, you will gain a good, practical sense of your current, most probable—and most satisfying to you—castability; the places where *you* believe you most easily fit in this collaborative art called drama.

3. The gist of the Orange Sheet is to get you to the point where you can assemble a short sales pitch or mission statement for yourself and your representatives so that, with their help, you can get out there and start marketing the magnificent and needed product that you are.

CHAPTER 13

Learning to Sidestep
Stage Fright

*Acting is half shame, half glory. Shame at exhibiting
yourself; glory when you can forget yourself.*

—John Gielgud

That little demon-monster; that horrible party-ruiner; that
nasty peace-of-mind destroyer and ruiner of all our fun—
stage fright! That thing that paralyzes us from getting up and
strutting our stuff and showing the world how absolutely wonderful we are. Anyone who has ever performed has at least some,
if not a far too intimate, acquaintance with that horrible, af-
flicting "Oh my God!" loss of a grasp on reality called stage
fright. It is fear and insecurity to the max. It is doubt, inhibition, and blockage to their absolute nth degrees. It is holy—or
unholy—terror. It is that feeling that you have swallowed your
teeth and lost your voice, that you are out of place and yet stick
out like a sore thumb, and that you are everything that everyone else would give everything they have to never be. You feel
disoriented and blind, subject to dissolution, and yet the un-
godly, unmerciful affliction will not dissolve or kill you, but,

119

toying with you, only keeps you at the emotional apex of raging terror that you are certain will never end.

Well, how do we avoid it? We certainly know how we get it—we dare to get up on stage. But how can we avoid it? *Can* we avoid it? Or is it something that we just have to live with or, more accurately, die a horrible death from, every performance night?

LIVE AND LET THE BUTTERFLIES LIVE

There seems to be a big difference between that maximum terror called stage fright and nerves, but in reality they are the same thing in different degrees. The fact is, like it or not, you can pretty much count on having nerves or stage fright to some degree whenever you get up to perform. It's part of the program. It comes with the territory. You are getting up there on stage baring your soul, baring your private parts—your weaknesses *and* your strengths (which you may feel may not exactly stand out). This is risky business because you are submitting yourself to judgment. I have never met a performer, in fact, who doesn't feel at least a little anxious when he or she gets up to perform. But you can manage it. That's the key. You can manage or mitigate the terror so it remains merely nerves. Say hello, though, to the butterflies in the stomach, the racing of the heart, the drops of perspiration, the quickening breath, because they are going to be with you throughout your career. Like an emotional entourage, the butterflies are going to accompany you every time you walk out on stage.

I think people exacerbate stage fright when they try to kid themselves by saying, "I'm not afraid!" I think you do better with stage fright when you admit that you are feeling it and allow it to be there. Inhale a little more deeply, exhale a little more fully, and open your psyche a little wider to accommodate those butterflies; and at the same time, focus your attention a little more sharply on the work at hand. That's my prescription. If you focus your energy on trying to get rid of the butterflies, which you can't really do, you will be taking your attention away from the work. But if you allow the butterflies to flutter and fly and turn your attention from them to your work, the stage fright itself, ironically, will have a beneficial effect on your performance. It will help lock your focus more sharply on your work.

❀ Affirmation

Hey, no sweat!

THE FOUR CAUSES OF STAGE FRIGHT

Why do we experience stage fright? Well, we want to be loved, we want to be approved of. We are standing there in front of the world with our clothes off, saying, "Here I am! What do you think?" The problem there, of course, is caring what other people think. We all know that. We've all been told by our parents and teachers and guardians, "Don't worry about what other people think about you; it's not important what other people think about you—it's only important what you think about yourself." We all know this. On a written test, we would all get it right. But, at least for now, we do care, which gives us stage fright. Why is it so difficult to manage it, though?

The **first** and greatest accomplice to stage fright is not having our motives in proper alignment. If we get up on stage for the purpose of being *thought* good instead of *being* good (although we still want to be thought good, as a by-product), if we're up there to get money instead of to do a good job (although we also want the money), and if we're up there to get glory instead of to glorify truth, then we're off our base and, naturally, we will be more likely to feel afraid. To feel secure,

121

our focus must be on the work itself, the acting, not on the by-products we might gain from it.

The **second** biggest cause of stage fright is not being prepared. Let me give you a little bit of comfort here. You will not be required to perform until you are ready. If somebody asks you to get up and sing a song, you can say no; you don't have to do it until you're ready to. In class, granted, ready or not, you do things to break inhibition. I ask my students to sing or dance on demand because I *want* them to feel that discomfort, I *want* them to experience what it feels like to go, "Oh, my God, I can't do it!" and feel like you're about to melt into a puddle and embarrass all reality by your very existence. But my students are in a safe environment with complete support from me, and we've already agreed that they will do what I ask because they know I want them to do all their "Oh, my God!" being terrified stuff in their sessions with me before they get out there on stage where their careers are at stake. While you are studying, you, too, may be asked to do things to gain experience and courage. But, as a general rule, you will not be required to perform a role until you've had plenty of time to prepare for that part in your armchair and at your rehearsals.

If, however, you don't take the time to thoroughly prepare and you get up on stage knowing that you are not ready to perform, you are going to feel terrified. You are going to have stage fright. But that self-sabotage, if it comes to that, will be your own doing; you will not ever be a "victim" of stage fright.

The **third** biggest cause of stage fright is lack of commitment. If you are not 100 percent committed to playing the role and playing it with all your energetic focus—if you are not clear about what you mean or do not fully mean it—then you are going to feel unstable in your created "reality" and will feel stage fright.

The **fourth** greatest cause of stage fright is loss of concentration on the work at hand. If your concentration wanders, you will naturally become afraid. You'll lose your place and forget your lines because you will have lost your anchor of truth within the created reality that, otherwise, would have kept you feeling safe and secure.

THE FIVE CURES

Now let's look at how we can lessen the degree to which we feel stage fright.

1. Align your motives properly. Remember that you are on stage to do a job. Don't get a big head. There's nothing special about you. You are fabulous and magnificent, that is true, but so is everyone else, and neither you nor any of the rest of us get the credit for that; that credit goes to our common creator. You are on stage to do a job, to serve. You are there to *be* the state of mind that you've signed up to be, to represent and embody a particular point of view. So get over yourself. Get over, "I'm so wonderful." Get over, "Boy, I could really get something good out of this," when by "good" you mean money and power. Instead, just be willing to *be* good.

2. Prepare. Be a good girl scout or boy scout and be prepared. Don't get up on stage without having done your homework. You are getting up there to shine, to be magnificent. But you are only going to *be* magnificent if you truly *are* magnificent in the work, which results from a process that begins in your armchair. Remember, most of your acting happens in your armchair—in your research, study, and your thinking about it and then in your rehearsals. The tip of the iceberg, the apotheosis, then comes into being on stage or in front of the camera when—and it is only *good* if—you have previously done all that groundwork. So prepare. Once you are thoroughly prepared, you will feel wonderful. You will feel secure and in your place and worthy of success. Consequently, you will have much less reason to be afraid.

3. Commit to the role. If you are going to play a schmo— a bad guy, a wimpy woman, a villain, an insecure slob—any character who, on the surface, doesn't seem to be anyone you or anyone else would strive to be, you still have to play that character with full commitment. Granted, it's easier to get behind playing the queen, or Joan of Arc, or Francis of Assisi, or any other great historical or mythical figure and commit to that; the ego latches on to that and says, "Yes, I'm very happy to be that state of mind!" But as an actor, you are doing a job of self-sacrifice; you lend your self—your body, mind, voice, and soul—to be used in the way that will best serve the play so that the audience can learn about life. You do that by committing to whatever role you're playing, whether you personally "like" the character or not. You must work until you are able to play him or her with understanding, compassion, tolerance, and love—a complete willingness to relate to and be this character to the best of your ability. And to the degree that you do that, you will feel less fear because you will feel more worthy of success.

4. Practice. Practice, practice, practice. Once you have aligned your motives, prepared, and have committed to the role, then practice until you feel the insecurity and doubt drain away. In proportion to your practice, there will be less and less fear until it's gone. Which is not to say that when you go on stage you won't still feel the butterflies; you will. Get comfortable with that. When you are standing in the wings ready to go on, say, "OK, butterflies, everybody here? All right, out we go!" But you won't feel that terrible sense of doubt, the feeling that you're not ready. Practice until you're secure, and then go get 'em!

5. Concentrate. Concentrate once you are out on stage. One of the benefits of acting, in fact, is that it teaches you to concentrate. You have to concentrate to succeed at anything in life, but even more so on stage. Discipline your thought to stay right in the moment. Concentrate on your subtext; concentrate on listening to what the other actors are saying; concentrate on your words and what you feel and what you mean; and do it fully in the spirit of service.

To the degree that you do all this, you will mitigate and manage stage fright. You will never "cure" it altogether, nor would you want to—you want the energy boost that it gives you.

✳ EXERCISE

Sing a song and dance as beautifully as you can. Listen for the insulting little demons in your head that say, "I can't do this" or "I'm not very good in this." Just note them. Not too tough, right? Good. Now find someone to do this exercise again in front of! Now it will be somewhat tougher. Do it, though, and note the mental demons and their attempts to insult you. Then dismiss them as beneath your consideration. The suggestion that you may need training is one thing; attempts to injure your self-esteem are quite another—they are to be summarily dismissed!

REVISITING VAMPING

When I'm working with a student and she forgets her line and becomes afraid, I tell her, with a merciless twinkle in my eye, "Suffer, baby!"

Yes, suffer. I want my students to deal with that feeling of forgetting their lines and discover they can come through it before they get on stage. You can't throw up your hands when you're on stage and say, "May I start over, please?," because no, little darling, you may not. Nor is that how it is in life. That "stop and start" stuff is allowed in acting only to the beginner. After the first few lessons, once the actor begins his monologue or scene he must go for it. If the actor loses his lines along the way, then he's got to improvise; he's got to vamp.

I spoke about vamping in chapter 6, but I think it warrents some revisiting here because it is such a helpful tool. The term *vamping* comes from the world of dancing. To catch her breath or prepare for a big move, the dancer stays in the same place for a minute, just going from one foot to another. The dancer is not traveling anywhere; she's just keeping the rhythm going, keeping the feeling going, before she moves forward again. It's like treading water in a pool.

In acting, vamping means that you continue to speak about what you were saying before you lost your place. Vamping occupies the part of the mind that is going, "Oh, my God! Oh, my God, I've forgotten my lines!" by making it extrapolate on what you have just said. The mind then automatically leads you right to where you need to be. You'll inadvertently say a word or phrase that cues your memory. I gave an example of this in chapter 6; here's another.

Let's say my lines are, "My grandfather had a ruby ring. From the time I was five years old, I grew up seeing that ring on his finger. Thirty years later, after he had been dead ten years, I asked my grandmother for his ring. But when I took it to a jeweler to have the stone set in a woman's ring, I discovered the ruby was a fake." Let's say I make it this far: "I asked my grandmother for his ring," and then I forget my lines. But I don't flip out; I employ the technique of vamping by talking more about what I've just said: "It was a beautiful ring, too. I remember two or three times when I was staying overnight with my grandparents I would see it sitting by itself on his nightstand and I would think, 'How can Daddy Blaine just leave it sitting out like that?'" Notice what is happening? My vamping is leading me right back on track. The phrase "just leave it sitting out like that" will cue me, and I'll remember, naturally, to say, "But when I took it to a jeweler . . . I discovered the ruby was a fake."

Vamping works because the mind never forgets anything. It will work for *you* if you trust your mind to lead you, which it will automatically do when, by vamping in place, you free it from the "Oh, my God, I've forgotten my lines!" fear.

You have to experience this a few times before you will trust this process, of course, and I recommend that you try it first in the safe harbor of an acting session or your own armchair. Once you do experience it, however, I know that you will be tickled pink to have this very valuable little safety net. You will then know that you will always be safe on stage, as long as you have done your homework. Nice, huh? You're welcome. Just send money.

※ EXERCISE

Purposefully "forget" your lines and then try vamping. Speak a moment more on what you have just said and find out for yourself that the technique works. That is the only way you will be able to trust your mind if you forget your lines on stage, but trustworthy it is. Try it!

If your motives are aligned, you have thoroughly prepared, you are committed to the role, you have practiced, your concentration and focus are sharp, *and* you know how to vamp on stage if you forget your lines, you will feel more secure and less stage fright than you might otherwise—all of which will free you to really let it rip on stage!

SUMMARY OF MAIN POINTS

1. Nerves and the terror called stage fright are defined by degrees.
2. You will always have nerves or butterflies before a performance—it comes with the territory and provides an energy boost. Unmanaged, stage fright can be debilitating, but it can be managed.
3. The four main causes of stage fright are:
   • The motive to get, rather than to give
   • Lack of preparation
   • Lack of commitment to the role
   • Loss of concentration

4. The five cures of stage fright are:
    - Proper alignment of your motives
    - Preparation
    - Commitment to the role
    - Practice
    - Concentration
5. Vamping in place is your safety net in case you forget your lines. It's very effective *if* you have done your homework.

CHAPTER 14

Breaking Down a Role

Acting is not for geniuses. It is for people who work step by step.

—Stella Adler

Twelve steps can be taken to break down any role into the character's desires and motives.

STEP ONE

First, in your armchair, read the entire play with an investigator's or researcher's eye—dispassionately, objectively, emotionally flat—*ten times!* That's right. Ten times. Avoid the temptation to make analyses or decisions too quickly. Certainly avoid the temptation to memorize so that you can hurry up and perform. What is the point of that? That's not acting. After you have read the play ten times, then read your part several times more, carefully. Read every word slowly with your miner's hat on to see what's going on.

What *is* going on? What is this play about? What are the different states of mind or points of view about life in this particular play and how do they interrelate? How do they play upon one another and what are the results of that interplay? What is your character's part in it? What are the themes of the play? What truths are being revealed, expounded, and concluded? Become very clear about all this, which you can do only if you take all the time that it requires.

STEP TWO

Second, working with your part, create the experiences that you are meant to have lived before your moments on stage. This is the "man-made lake, but a lake all the same" idea. When something is meant to have happened in your character's past that you must then later relate on stage, such as, "Yesterday I went out to the pasture and saw the most beautiful horse," you must first, in your armchair, create the "reality" of that memory. You do that by imagining all the elements and aspects of that experience. Imagine the horse. Imagine the pasture. Imagine how you got there, why you went, what you were wearing, the time of the day, the weather, the way you felt when you first saw the horse, the interchange between you and the horse, the thoughts you were having while you were there, and so on. Imagine as much as *you* deem necessary to accept it as a "real" experience, so that when you later relate the experience to your scene partner during your performances on stage, you will speak of it as though it truly happened, even though it happened only in your mind. The audience will then believe that it is real as well.

STEP THREE

The third tool for breaking down a role is assigning substitutions. Using your own experience, cast the play in your mind. If you are going to be talking about an Uncle Ted or to an Aunt Mildred, select real faces and real personalities from your past to embody these character blueprints. This way, as you start your research and rehearse, you will be creating for yourself a more solid reality than if these characters remained nebulous and nonspecific. After you have assigned faces to the characters, plug in real places and events that you can easily relate to from your own experiences. This also will make it more believable to your audience.

STEP FOUR

Next, empathize. The main purpose of using things from your life—your past, your experience—is that doing so will spark in you greater emotional involvement with what is going on in the drama. Remember, the actor's job, on stage or in front of the camera, is to feel emotion. You must be able to understand and empathize with what your character is assigned to be feeling. You do that by using your own life and by realizing that other people are dealing with the same issues that your character is, so that by the time you have created your character, you will be feeling these feelings.

This is a grand work, isn't it? It's not all fun and games. It is serious and powerful work, the purpose of which is to move us all a little closer to heaven.

STEP FIVE

Fifth, get the rhythm or music of your character's words in your mouth. When we speak during our everyday interchanges with one another, our feelings orchestrate our thoughts, then our words. The sounds of the words we choose, the way we string our words together and deliver them are all an effect of our feelings. We say things in the way that we feel them and there is always a sense of music to our expression. Find that musicality in the words of your character, because that musicality was

131

initially in the mind of the writer when he or she wrote them; you will need it and want it when you perform or channel your character's point of view to your audience. This will help you to communicate in a way that your audience will find intellectually and emotionally satisfying. It's as if you are returning to the point of the play's origin in the mind of the writer, revisiting his or her mind-set, discovering and reliving what he or she was feeling when the words were first spoken in the playwright's mind by the characters, which you can then most purely deliver for your audience.

STEP SIX

After you have become clear about the writer's feelings and the meaning behind every word in the play, take over: make sure that *you* have a meaning for everything that *you*, as the character, say and do and that it all makes perfect sense to *you*. The purpose for this, of course, is that it's going to be your butt out there on stage performing, not the playwright's. To feel stable, solid, and secure, to do a good job and enjoy acting, you have to feel real. And the only way you can feel real is to absolutely, 100 percent, no fooling around mean every little thing that you say—not to mention every big one. After all your research and prep, it finally comes down to the fact that you, the actor, must rely on your own understanding of life to support what you say and do.

STEP SEVEN

Allow your character to become "opinionated." If I say, "I think you're handsome," I also have a feeling about that. I may be glad that I think you're handsome, because I love you. Or I might wish I didn't, because I also believe you are a bad man.

132

You must have an opinion on everything that you, as the character, say, because that's how it is in life. In fact, the judgments that audience members perceive you, as the character, have about what you are saying communicate more information to them than the words you speak.

"This is my husband. He is a salesman" is flat information; it tells us nothing about the human condition. But the way the actress speaks those words tells us whether or not she's pleased that the man is her husband and whether or not she's pleased that he is a salesman, as well as what she thinks his chances for success are. That is what acting is about. Stanislavski said, "The fact that the hero of a play kills himself is not so important as the inner reason for his suicide."

STEP EIGHT

By this time, if you have done the work in the previous seven steps, you should be equipped to recognize and draw conclusions about the most crucial aspect of the play: the governing desires and objectives of each of the play's characters. The interplay of those desires is the heart of any play.

For example, *Casablanca* is not about World War II, although that was its backdrop. *Casablanca* is about two lovers who both, in their own ways, rise to the challenge of choosing loyalty over personal desire.

The Visit is not about the greedy members of a small town, but about an ostracized woman who, now wealthy, returns to her past and, through financial seduction, reduces her tormentors to a level far below that for which they ostracized her, proving to herself, and to them, that they were never better than she was.

No Exit is not about three people who end up sharing a hotel room together. It's about the hell their conflicting states of mind create for each of them, when forced to share company for eternity.

In all three instances, more important than the setting, the plot, or even the characters themselves is the play, or interplay, of the desires and objectives of those characters. So delve deeply and determine clearly the exact nature of the interplay between the desires of the characters in your stage or screenplay.

STEP NINE

Once you have determined the main governing motives and desires of all the characters in your play and how they interact, focus on what you, as your character, want, and go after it. Play your action with the shameless single-pointedness of mind of a hungry kitten that simply will not shut up until her mistress stops what she is doing and feeds her. Every few lines, remind yourself what you're after, what you want, and let that—your governing motive or desire within the play—color with feeling, meaning, and opinion, all that you say and do. And let it determine *the way* that you say and do what you do. That way, when you are performing, we, the audience, will understand your point of view and aims and how they interrelate with those of the other characters in the play.

STEP TEN

Next, map out your character's emotional journey. See where your character is up, down, or flat. Define those ups and downs by giving them specific *emotion names:* "I'm feeling jealous here, I'm feeling joyful there, then I dip down into jealousy again, and then, sparked by another character's funny remark, I dump the jealousy and adopt a false attitude of confidence." That is your character's emotional journey. This specific emotional definition will help you remember where you are if you forget your lines during a performance.

STEP ELEVEN

Once you have mapped out your emotional journey, you then need to plug in your subtext. What thoughts are you thinking between your lines? What double or hidden meanings do you have behind your words? We always have thoughts before, between, and after the things we say out loud. In acting, it is crucial to carefully select these subtext thoughts because, to a great degree, they constitute and support our feelings and, consequently, motivate and color the way our words come out. After all, that's how it is in life. And, as in life, so on stage or in front of the camera. But how do we find or create these underlying thoughts?

The best way is to improvise. Stand up, lie down, move around, flail your arms, speak your lines through a straw—whatever it takes. Put the entire script into your own words. Expand on your lines, extrapolate, put blocks of text into one concise phrase. Talk about and around what you've said, explain what you mean. Say nothing and put your entire speech into one physical gesture. Fool around and see what emerges.

This is all work that you first do by yourself—at home in your armchair or bathtub or some place where you will not be disturbed—before you ever start to rehearse with your play partners. Then you do it all again with your acting partners. As you do it, the work will deepen and you will become more knowledgeable and comfortable. Then when you return to the script itself, you will find you have made it *yours*.

STEP TWELVE

Now that you've gotten everything in place exactly the way that you want it and are able to say things exactly the way you mean them, now that nothing has escaped you, now that everything that you are feeling and saying and doing is done for a purpose motivated by your inner, conscious reasoning—then, and *only* then, do you begin to memorize. *Now* you can memorize those lines! Also memorize your subtext, the selected between-the-spoken-lines thoughts that motivate and support your lines. Get it down pat, which will be nearly effortless if you have done the previous steps; you will have avoided the stress that ordinarily comes with straight memorization. And then you must simply practice, practice, practice!

NOW, DO IT!

At the beginning of this book we made an agreement. We agreed that we would all consider ourselves actors: Actors Anonymous. We agreed to read this book, at least the first time, from the standpoint of being an actor. I asked you to do this because I believed this would give you a more immediate visceral insight into the ideas herein—ideas that can be applied to any area of creative endeavor.

Now I'm going to ask you to take it one step further. Agree, if you will, not only to continue reading this book as an actor, but actually *be* an actor—at least for the time it takes you to finish reading this book. Get a play that you like and that has a character in it that you like and—if for only this one time in your life—sit in your armchair and, applying the previous twelve steps, break down the role for yourself. Why not? It'll be fun. Try it. You might like it. You might *love* it. You might find you have a knack for it. Hey, stranger things have happened! And then, when you are comfortable with your part and have a good sense of what's happening, call some of your friends and say, "You know, just for the heck of it, why don't we all get together and read this play?" Then try working on it together, one scene at a time. You know what that will mean, don't you? It will mean you'll be working on a play! And before long, if you continue to enjoy doing it, you might even decide to produce it. Why not? You might get one hell of a bang out of it!

❀ *Affirmation*

I am as intelligent and talented as the greatest thinkers and artists the world has ever known.

SUMMARY OF MAIN POINTS

1. In breaking down a role, first read the play ten times.
2. In your armchair create the experiences your character will later retell on stage.
3. Assign substitutions.
4. Relate to, or identify with, the experiences of your character.
5. Get the rhythm or music of the words of your character in your mouth.
6. Be sure that you have a clear meaning for everything your character says and does.
7. Allow your character to become opinionated.
8. Determine and draw conclusions about the governing desires and objectives of each of the play's characters.
9. Focus on your own character's desires and objectives and go after them.
10. Map out your character's emotional journey.
11. Improvise and plug in your subtext.
12. Memorize your lines.

CHAPTER 15

The Art and Craft of Cold Reading

Your lines should sound like spontaneous conversation, not like acting at all. And that comes from actively listening.

—Michael Caine

It is imperative for the actor to have a good, solid, effective cold-reading technique because it is through either cold reading or performing a monologue that the actor gets the job—and 90 percent of the time it's through cold reading. You want a tried-and-true technique you can rely on to not only get you through it, but to make you shine.

When a producer or director is having an actor read for a part, he or she doesn't expect the actor to nail the reading dead on. Any good director will know that nailing a part takes time and preparation, so he won't expect you to be at performance level. What he is looking for during a cold reading is an assurance that you will be able to do the part when the time comes. The only way a director is going to know that is if he sees some solid interaction between you and the other actor you're reading with. And he can only see that interaction if you look off the page into the eyes of your scene partner when you are speaking. That's where my cold-reading technique comes in.

THE LOGISTICS OF AUDITIONING

Jane Fonda said, "The most important thing to remember when auditioning is to relax!" Following a few simple guidelines will help you to do that.

First of all, get the sides early and *practice*! The sides are the pages that you will be reading in the audition. If you have an agent and access to a fax machine, you can usually get the sides the day before the audition because the casting director, upon request, will have faxed the sides to your agent when he or she booked the audition, and your agent can then fax them to you. If you can't, arrive at your audition an hour early. Give yourself enough time to do essentially what you would do in your armchair. Find a corner and then, at 20 percent volume—just loud enough for you to hear yourself—read the part slowly ten times aloud. The first few times you'll be reading it just to see what's in there, what's going on between the characters, and to hear the musicality of the dialogue. Then read it a few more times to gain familiarity with it. Then commit what you can to memory. But don't put much effort into memorization; it's not usually expected that you memorize your lines for an audition. If it is, you will have been advised. Nonetheless, certain phrases or short sentences may easily fall into place in your memory, and if they do, that will add to your comfort with the material. The important thing, though, is to stay centered, calm, and relaxed as much as possible and to trust your instincts about the part.

Once you're clear and feel pretty confident about what you're saying and the way you want to say it, then look around the waiting area for an actor who looks like he or she is the type that might be reading opposite to you. In other words, if one part calls for a woman of twenty and the other for a woman of forty-five and you are twenty, look for a woman who *obviously* will be reading for the part of the forty-five-year-old. Be careful about this, though! You might ask the forty-five-year-old what part she's reading for and let her blush with delight that there was even any question about it. Then ask her if she would like to read the scene with you for practice. This has a marvelous twofold effect: it prepares and grounds you both, plus it increases your sense of dominion. *You* made this happen, and now you are feeling much more ready for your audition.

❀ *Affirmation*

> *I am calm, cool, collected, and ready for action! Let me at it!*

THE AUDITION IS THE REAL THING

"There are no rehearsals in life." Whoever first said that was right. Life is the real thing. It is happening *now*. You don't get to "take it once more from the top." You have to give it your best shot in this moment because this is the only shot you are ever going to get to take action in this moment. Not that life is going to end—but neither is it going to start over again!

The same dynamic applies to actors on the stage. You don't get to start over in the middle of a performance. You don't get to say to your audience, "Excuse me, folks. Let me try that again." No. You do the best you can, and if you blow it, you go on from there.

For that reason, I believe the actor should consider every audition to be a performance. You may not be off-book (have the script memorized), but when it is your turn to audition, you are *on*! You are performing and you are the star. The "run" may last only one or two minutes and you may be playing to a house of only one, but during that run you are the star of the show.

And you should *act* accordingly, taking both yourself and your performance seriously. Working this way delivers you from the mind-set of hope and supplication and seats you in your artistic integrity and authority, which helps you to concentrate and do a good job.

❊ Affirmation

> *I did it! I did it my way and I did it well! Tangible progress can't help but result! Thank you, life.*

MY TECHNIQUE

By the time you will have been called in to actually audition, you will have prepared and rehearsed enough so that you will probably have inadvertently memorized some of your lines. Again, it's fine if you have and it's fine if you haven't. My technique calls for you to behave the same way in either case. Just be sure that by the time you read, you have become thoroughly familiar with the words and their phrasing so that, by a quick glance at the script, you will be able to roll them off the tip of your tongue effortlessly.

Silently, to yourself—and this requires deep concentration in an audition when the tension is higher than normal—read a short sentence, or a phrase that breaks at a natural point (at an *and*, a *but*, or a comma), then look at your scene partner and say it. Then look back down at your script for the next sentence or phrase portion thereof, capture it, then look up at your partner and say it. That's it. Simple. But not easy.

What you are doing is capturing a portion of the dialogue into your short-term memory, going with your instincts on what it means, and delivering it with that meaning to your partner. But when you are speaking, you are speaking *off the page*, which allows you to make eye contact and interact with your partner and shows your prospective employers what it will be like if they hire you for the part.

This technique has the added benefit of making you slow down and relax every time you deliver a line, because unless you do relax, you won't be able to concentrate enough to capture the line into your short-term memory. I encourage you to check your line before you say it, whether you have "memorized" it or not, however. Use the script. Tension will be high and you won't have had time to get it deeply enough into memory for a comfortable performance anyway, so give yourself a break. Instead of having to search your memory for a line, glance at the page, then use your effort to focus on meaning what you are saying. This will serve you better, because you don't get the cookie in acting for memorization; you get it for feeling the feelings.

Another thing: More important than the lines you will be reading is the relationship between you and your scene partner. You need to concentrate and *listen* to what your scene partner says *first*, before you *then* react to him or her. So be courageous. You don't have to know what your next line is; it's better if you don't. You just have to have your finger in place on the page so you can find your next line after your partner has said his line and you have had a natural reaction to it. Then look down and find the line, which, 90 percent of the time will agree with your own impulse. Since there is one common consciousness, the way you respond and the way the playwright wrote your character to respond will probably be pretty much the same. So stay on the edge, in the moment, and trust your instincts.

PRACTICE THE TECHNIQUE IN YOUR ARMCHAIR

This technique of silently reading a line, then looking up and saying it takes practice. Practice it at home in your armchair. It will take some getting used to, but once you get it down, the benefits will be skill, confidence, and the ability to do more act-ing during the audition because you will be free to interact more with your partner. And you will have found a way to avoid that horrible head-up-and-down-every-few-words action that makes everyone in the room seasick! Best of all, this technique will en-able you to behave the most naturally and—very best of all—will make the auditioning experience more fun and satisfying to you.

Yes, but what about the time it takes to read silently? Shouldn't we hurry up? In a word, no! "Excuse me for being here. I'll just hurry and get off the stage so someone important can come on." No. It's your moment. You are the star, so shine. Because, believe me, the next guy or gal waiting will certainly try to. Yes, this technique may take a few silent seconds between lines but the others in the room will quickly adjust to your rhythm, and the benefits of this technique make the short wait well worth it. Besides, they're used to waiting for actors. Ac-tors are the last ones to get ready on a set. Everyone waits for the actor before the director finally says action, and for good reason. The actor's job is the most important one. He or she lives and conveys the feelings—the soul—of the drama, for which, lest we forget, the actor also gets paid the most hand-somely. So remember who you are and what you have to do here. Your performance will more than justify the technique and, I promise, you will get no complaints. Especially from your scene partner; a benefit to him of this technique is that it makes you a more generous partner because it frees you to look and lis-ten to him when he is speaking his lines; this helps him to be-lieve them.

※ EXERCISE

Practice my technique of cold reading. Use a scene, a mono-logue, or any piece of prose or poetry text. Stay with it until you've got it. Build this skill methodically, and it will serve

143

you in good stead when the stakes, and the vibrating frequency of your nerves, are higher!

SUMMARY OF MAIN POINTS

1. It is imperative for an actor to have a good, solid cold-reading technique because a director can see if an actor will be able to do a role only if the actor is able to look off the page into the eyes of his or her scene partner.
2. The cold-reading technique described in this chapter allows the actor to do this. The technique consists of silently reading a short sentence or a phrase, then looking up and saying it to your scene partner with your eyes *off the page*.
3. Consider the audition the real thing—a performance—even if for a run of only a minute! Treat it accordingly.
4. Prepare yourself fully; then audition *your* way.

Part III

OVERCOMING
THE OBSTACLES
TO DOING IT

*Encouragement
and the
Business of Acting*

CHAPTER 16

The Biz

There are two businesses in this world: the business you're in and show business.

—Shirley MacLaine

Acting is a business. It is an art and a calling, but it is also a business. And you maximize the art of acting by first accepting it as a business. Because when you approach acting as a business, you will deal with it much differently than if you were thinking about it as just something you wanted to do. When you choose to make money acting, you will begin to develop a business strategy regarding it, and that is crucial to your success as an actor.

You can see how important it is, then, for the actor to know what his or her product is and can do—where, in casting, it fits in the world of acting. To make a living acting, his or her acting—like any other product—has to fit a market niche that is recognizable and appreciated by those to whom he or she applies for employment.

THE NECESSARY STEPS

A guy prays to win the lottery. Every day for months he prays, "Please, God, let me win the lottery," but nothing ever happens. One day he changes his prayer, "Please, God, tell me what I should do so I can win the lottery." He listens hard and, sure enough, a voice whispers in his ear, "Buy a lottery ticket."

We, too, have to take the necessary steps and do the day-to-day business groundwork in our acting careers, and a lot of legwork needs to be done in the business of acting. Most often, it takes a long time before our work comes to fruition. So the sooner we get on with it, the better.

※ EXERCISE

Write ten things you think you can do right now to further your business of acting. Just listen to yourself. Trust your instincts and write what comes to you.

1. _____
2. _____
3. _____
4. _____
5. _____
6. _____
7. _____
8. _____
9. _____
10. _____

Now, commit to doing at least three of them, beginning tomorrow.

A GOOD HEAD SHOT

The first thing you need is a good head shot. Was that on your list? People try to save money on their head shots. This is understandable since money is usually tight when an actor is starting out. But in acting your head shot is your calling card. You need a *good* one. When you compare your cost of doing business to that of many other business start-ups, you don't really have much to complain about. Others pay hundreds of thousands on research, development, and marketing. For you, it's coaching, photographs, résumés, cosmetics, and a little wardrobe. It's minimal. So don't skimp on the cost of a good head shot. When you are starting out as an actor, that, more than anything else, is what causes casting directors to call you in to audition. That's not to say you can't get a good one unless you pay lots of money for it, but don't settle for a head shot unless you are really satisfied with it.

HOW DO YOU GET A GOOD HEAD SHOT?

Take a look at the head shots of other actors. If you find one you like, ask who shot it. If you have access to any agents or casting directors, ask them what they think constitutes a good head shot and to show you one or two they think are good and tell you why. Ask them for recommendations for a good photographer. Interview prospective photographers; look at their portfolios and see if the chemistry is good between you. A good photographer is like a good lover; he or she makes you feel safe enough to flirt with the camera and reveal your most attractive self. Make sure the photographer you select will be able to do that for you.

After you select a photographer and have your pictures taken, then take the proofs to people you think know a good head shot when they see one (other actors, casting directors, agents, acting coaches) and get their vote as to which shot you should select to be your head shot. Ultimately, though, like everything in your work and your life, it is your call: you have to make the decision. But don't be hasty. You are going to live with this decision for a while, so taking an extra week or two is not going to kill you. Take the time necessary to get a good, *effective* head shot.

The styles of head shots change with the times. Sometimes, just head and shoulders seems to be in; other times three-quarter body shots are more popular. Usually, an actor needs two different head shots: a smiling shot for commercials and another more serious pose for theatrical and film work. However, some actors use only one, which can be sufficient if the shot is a good blend of the two. One tip, though: The most important facial feature in any head shot is the eyes. You want to have a good, dead-on, fully connecting gaze of the eyes. And there is nothing wrong with having your photograph touched up so you get a little sparkle in the eyes, either, if it's not there already.

THE TWO MAIN USES OF THE HEAD SHOT

The head shot has two main purposes. First, it helps you to get an agent. You will send out a mailing of head shots and résumés, along with a short cover letter stating that you are looking for representation, to a list of agents. Apart from your experience listed on your résumé, which in the beginning is not as strong as it will be later, it is your head shot more than anything that will spark an agent's interest in calling you in for an interview.

Second, once you have secured an agent, he or she will begin submitting copies of your head shot and résumé to casting directors. It is from your head shots and résumés that casting directors will, or will not, select you to audition. Once you do secure an agent, however, he or she may ask you to have additional pictures taken by a photographer that he or she uses and trusts. But again, that cost of doing business is negligible—especially since you will now have progressed to the point where you have an agent! It's something you are just going to have to get used to; you'll probably need new photos once a year for the rest of your acting life. Do it. The value of a good head shot far exceeds the cost.

YOUR RÉSUMÉ

Your résumé must be a good résumé. Does that surprise you? I didn't think it would. But how do you make it good if you're a beginner and you haven't really done much? If you're a newcomer, you'll want to be creative about your résumé. Short and sweet and creative. A casting director is going to give your head shot about three seconds of his or her time, and your résumé about two. That's five seconds altogether. "How does she look?" and "What has she done?" Those are the two questions the casting director will ask him- or herself. The answer to the first should be obvious: quirky, homegrown, funny, unique, pretty, scary, cool—any of the qualities you have chosen to represent you as your product in your head shot. The answer to the second, if possible, should be "lots." But until it is, let it be what it is, enhanced by a little creativity. And have it follow the standard layout, which the following sample résumés will illustrate. (Note that Résumé 1 is constructed to show that this actor works a lot and in big roles. If he'd done all this, he'd be a household name and wouldn't need a résumé!)

RÉSUMÉ 1 (HIGHLY EXPERIENCED)

SAG, AFTRA   6 ft 1 in/180 lbs.
EQUITY   dark brn/blue

THEATER

Seven Brides for Seven Brothers	Jed	Joseph Papp Theatre
The Iceman Cometh	Hickey	Manhattan Theatre Club
Long Day's Journey into Night	Jamie	Actors Studio
True West	Lee	Roundabout Theatre
The King and I	King	Golden Theatre
Death of a Salesman	Willie Loman	Martin Beck Theatre
Sweet Bird of Youth	Chance	Marquis Theatre
A Streetcar Named Desire	Stanley Kowalski	Neil Simon Theatre

FILM

Amadeus	Mozart	Thorn/EMI
Gandhi	Gandhi	Columbia
Jerry Maguire	Maguire	Tri Star
The Godfather	Vito Corleone	Paramount
Blue Velvet	Frank	Lorimar
The Big Chill	Nick	MCA/UA
Taxi Driver	Travis Bickle	Columbia
Ghost	Sam	Paramount

TELEVISION

Days of Our Lives	One of the leads	NBC
The Bold and the Beautiful	One of the leads	CBS
The West Wing	Platt	NBC
Law and Order	Benson	NBC
The Practice	Bobby	ABC

COMMERCIALS—list on request

TRAINING

Charles Conrad, Roy London, Lorrie Hull, Robert Modica, Kathryn Bild

SPECIAL SKILLS

Skydiving, race-car driving, deep-sea diving, tennis, polo, sharpshooting, singing, dancing, saving the world

RÉSUMÉ 2 (MODERATELY EXPERIENCED)

SAG Eligible   5 ft 6 in/125 lbs.

                                                              Blonde/Blue

THEATER

27 Brides . . . 957 Poems	Bride	Ruckus Ensemble
Danny and the Deep Blue Sea	Roberta	Odyssey Theatre/LA

FILM

Remarkable Women	Trudy	USC Grad Film
An All-Consuming Passion	Guard	American Film Institute
Jerry Maguire	Tess	Tri Star

TELEVISION

Television Parts	Various roles	NBC
Quick 'n Easy	Chef De Pray	Warner/Amex
Saturday Night Live	Featured	NBC

VIDEO

Comedy Shorts	Various roles	DaBoy Productions
Toto	Cowgirl	Pacific Arts

COMMERCIALS

Ivory Liquid, GTE, Knudsen Yogurt

SINGING

Clubs, recordings

TRAINING

Stella Adler, HB Studios, Bob Mathews

RÉSUMÉ 3 (INEXPERIENCED)

5 ft 11 in/192 lbs.

Brown/Brown

THEATER

Oklahoma	Chorus	Pierce Junior College

FILM

Three Guys Without a Clue	Mike	Independent short

TELEVISION

The Rosie O'Donnell Show	Audience member

TRAINING
Karen Whieland, Pierce Junior College Drama Department

SPECIAL SKILLS
Juggling, making rude noises with different body parts

Notice that in all three examples—and this is a good rule of thumb—the categories were listed in the following order: theater, film, television, commercials, training, and then your particular special talents (two or three). That's standard. And remember, brevity is considered a virtue by agents and casting directors. They look at hundreds of head shots and résumés each week. They don't want an epic. They just want to know if you're capable as an actor—if you can play the part if they call you in and you are hired.

AND A SHORT COVER LETTER

You've got a fabulous head shot that shows the magic in your eyes and a résumé attached to the back of it that simply and to the point informs the agent that you are able to handle an acting job. That leaves the cover letter.

Agents are busy. I recently had a conversation with Bill Robinson, one of the seven founding agents at ICM, whose clients include Carol Burnett and James Gardner. In addition to affirming that it is imperative for an actor to have a drop-dead, attention-getting head shot, Bill stressed that throughout an actor's career—in the beginning and when he becomes a star—it is important that he never take any more of an agent's time than he absolutely needs. He added that it was also important to express appreciation for the time the agent does give you. That's his opinion, of course, but it's only good business. So make the cover letter that accompanies your head shot and résumé short and to the point. Here are two examples:

Dear Mac:
I am seeking representation for commercials—for on-camera and voice-over.

Thank you,
[Your name.]

Dear Mary:

I am new to New York and am seeking new representation for MP/TV and theater, please. I have recently signed with Cunningham for commercials.

Thank you for your consideration.
[Your name.]

That's it. Which brings me to another point: You want one agency for commercials—for on-camera and/or voice-over work—and one for legit, which includes motion pictures, television, and theater. Make sure that whichever you are looking for is specified in your cover letter, as shown above.

Again, keep it short and to the point. Don't spend any time telling them how great you are and how much money you're going to make them. They've heard it all before. If there is something you truly think they should know, fine. But don't blow your horn or try to be clever. It won't work. Let your picture and résumé make your pitch for you. That's why your head shot has got to be great—that and your résumé will get you in the door.

Once you've got a good head shot, résumé, and short cover letter, congratulate yourself. That, in itself, is a huge achievement. Next, purchase a published list of agents and then begin submitting your head shots, résumés, and letters by mail to the agents who seem right for you. In chapter 20 I'll tell you exactly how to go about selecting agents and how—and how often—to submit to them. But first things first. *First* concentrate on getting a drop-dead head shot!

DO YOUR SPIRITUAL WORK DAILY

Throughout this process and once your pictures and résumés are in the pipeline, is there anything you can do mentally to help your efforts succeed? You bet.

Our personal efforts and steps are important and none should be hurried or dismissed. But the most crucial thing to do in the business of acting is to have your daily business meeting with your source. When you first open your eyes in the morning, affirm for yourself your place, identity, and condition, as well as your function in the world. Realize where you are. You are not in Hollywood, you are not in New York. You are not in this business, and you are not in a quandary. You are in the kingdom of heaven—the realm of consciousness—so claim that. Once you have established your true place, establish your true identity as the expression of perfect life, and then the ongoing, immutable condition of that identity.

It is so important every day to establish for yourself the correct sense of where and who you really are, because otherwise you are going to start believing you are where and who you are *not*; and then before long you will start acting like it. No. You are, and exist to be, the perfect manifestation of all that is magnificent. That is your heritage, that is your identity, that is your ongoing condition and your function—forever. Affirm for yourself the spiritual laws that are operating in this place, consciousness, and see that your success in all your ventures, therefore, must be inevitable.

EXERCISE

Complete the following sentences, quickly, with whatever first pops into your head.

1. **When I don't treat my desires with respect,**

   ____.

2. **In order to take my desires more seriously,**

   ____.

3. **If I pay more attention to my desires today,**

   ____.

CONSIDER YOURSELF A PLAYER

Once you have consciously remembered and reclaimed what is true about you spiritually, then take a few moments to consider yourself a player on the field of acting.

"Oh, I wish I could be a player! I wish I could get out there (or in there, or up there) and play! I want to do it too, not just watch others do it. I want to be a player!"

Know the feeling? It's a powerful ambitious impulse that gets us off the sidelines onto the playing field and keeps us in there swinging. It's a good impulse and when we act on it, it feels great. But when you feel like you're *not* a player, you feel like an outsider standing with your nose pressed against the windowpane. You feel out of it. You make phone calls, but nobody takes them and nobody calls you back. It seems like everybody has a deal but you. Everybody is starring in a play, a film, a sitcom, or has just booked a commercial but you. You can't even get arrested. If you took off all your clothes in the middle of Grand Central Station and yelled "Take me!," everyone would walk by and ignore you.

Everyone wants to be a player. To be taken seriously, to be respected, to be valued. It's natural. We want everybody—from Madonna to the Pope—to take our phone call or return it the same damn day! After all, *you* know who you are, *you* know you have something to give, and you just want the chance to give it. You want to be chosen as a player, and there's nothing wrong with that. But don't forget who is doing the choosing.

Nothing is more frustrating when you are chomping at the bit to play than not being able to even get out onto the field. In the case of acting (unless you are producing your own shows), that frustration is aggravated by your dependence on other people to hire you in order for you to get your opportunities to express your talents—not to mention make a living. When things are not going well, you may feel at the mercy of those other people. But you are not; you are on assignment in this career workshop on this pilgrimage. And although it is true that it will be others who will actually hire you, they, too, are on assignment. They will be prompted to hire you once *you* take *yourself* seriously. That's the key. Consider *yourself* a player—a valuable player—then trust life to inspire others to take you seriously as well.

THE EARTH SANDBOX

The glorious truth is, if you are on the Earth at this time—in the Earth sandbox, as it were—then you *are* a player. We're on the playground; we're *players*! That's right! If we are here at this point, at this time, then we are sanctioned players—just as much as Michael Jordan, Tiger Woods, Barbra Streisand, Leonardo DiCaprio, or anybody else is. We have the God-given right to be here and play in the game, no matter what anybody else happens to think about it. And our playmates in the acting game—whether they are movie stars, studio heads, or bigtime directors—*have* to take us seriously because God says so! Our common parent, coach, and boss says we get to play, and nobody else has the right or the ability to keep us from playing.

To activate that truth in your experience, someone has to acknowledge and accept it, though. Who would that be, do you think? Right! *You* do. It is always *us*. That's what gives us the opportunity to get up to bat—the fact that we *take* it. We say, "We, gol-dang it, are players!" and we get out there and we assert our selves, our talents, and our rights.

We do all this in modest degrees, however. We are faced with what seem to be huge challenges and achieve small victories. But that's beautiful because that's the way life is, for us and for most of the characters we play. Flowers and fruit grow a little bit each day, and so do people. And when we sign up for the long haul and make sure that we do our little bit every day—in our acting and in whatever else we choose—we succeed.

✳ EXERCISE

Please write five affirmations, five true statements about the quality and value of your artistic assets. If you are uncertain whether or not they are true, write what you would like to be true.

1. _____
2. _____
3. _____
4. _____
5. _____

The statements you have written above are true—even the ones you thought you only wished to be so. It is impossible to make a positive statement—broken down to its essence—that is not true about yourself.

THE POSITIVE EFFECTS OF RIGHT THINKING

When we think about ourselves as players, we conduct ourselves just a little differently. When we remember that we are needed, wanted, and appreciated, and then call up for an interview or a meeting or go in for an audition, we're not quite as apologetic or supplicantlike as we may otherwise have been. We're more confident, more at ease, and we are taken a bit more seriously by others. This, happily, is in striking contrast to those bad days when you call someone important and feel like saying, "It's only me. You probably don't want to talk to me. I don't blame you. Never mind. Sorry to bother you."

When you know you are a player, you call up and you're in your power. You have something to offer and you know it. And when they hit you with, "Uh, who are you?" or "Is your movie financed yet?" or "Name ten top movies you have already starred in"—because they, bless their jaded little hearts, are buying into that terrible showbiz mesmerism that says you

159

have to be in the top 1 percent to be of any value—you can swat all that away with a wave of your hand as if it were one little harmless gnat.

You are a player—in the *big* game as well as in the little ones. You see through all that fear. You will not fall prey to feeling insecure because you are not Steven Spielberg or Barbra Streisand yet—and never will be. You are who you are, and *right now* you have as much to offer as Spielberg or Streisand, and they would be the first people to tell you so. Your understanding of this fact will diffuse any resistance you encounter and you will come across with the confidence, intelligence, love, and talent that you possess in abundance. Sure, it costs a lot of money to mount a production. People will want to assure themselves that you are a worthy bet. But when *you* know that you are worthy, that truth will shine bright in the minds of others.

SUMMARY OF MAIN POINTS

1. You maximize the art of acting by first accepting that acting is also a business.
2. In acting, your head shot is your calling card. You need a good one!
3. Your head shot has two main purposes. The first is to secure a good agent(s); the second is to get the attention of casting directors so they will call you in to audition.
4. Your résumé must be good. If you are a newcomer, then you will have to be creative in the construction of your résumé. Include something to make them realize you are experienced enough in other areas so that, naturally, if given the chance, you will shine as an actor.
5. Support your efforts with trust and confidence. This comes from doing your daily spiritual work and considering yourself a player equal to everyone else on the field. Realize that you as supply, by spiritual law, are in demand, and that you are a worthy bet in the game.

CHAPTER 17

Playing by the Spiritual Rules

We are ourselves creations. And we, in turn, are meant to continue creativity by being creative ourselves.

—Julia Cameron

Of course you want to play by the rules, don't you? You don't? Why not? There's a rebel in us who says, "I am exempt from the rules. I may break the rules." But why would you want to break them? You want to be exempt from or break the rules if the rules don't serve you, if they limit you in some way.

If you are playing by rules that are based on the false beliefs of evil and scarcity, then naturally you will not only want to, but have the divine right to break those rules. But you are not truly bound by such rules anyway and never have been. Even the laws of the land won't bind you if you do not willingly submit to them; you may break any of the laws of the land. If you're caught breaking them, you may pay a penalty but you don't *have* to follow them.

However, spiritual rules exist that really *are* rules. They are rules or principles by which we are truly and inextricably bound; laws that can't be broken. The fortunate thing about these rules of the game of life is that they are good, beneficial, life-supportive—*you* supportive—rules that, on consideration, no one would want to break.

THE SPIRITUAL PRINCIPLES

1. The Principle of the Coincidence of Supply and Demand (Life Is in Perfect Balance). Life is intelligent. There is no supply that is not demanded. Nor is there any demand that is not already supplied. Because life is love expressed, supply and demand are *coincident*. Regarding your acting, this means that because you have the desire and the ability to act, you also have the opportunity to act. With this law, as with all spiritual laws, before we can see it operating in our lives, we must understand and accept it.

Society, however, often gives us a very different message about supply and demand. It tells you, "You have more debt than means to meet it. Life, itself, is running out, let alone time! What you have as supply, the world does not want. There are no opportunities for you." Which will you choose? We've often accepted the message of limitation, haven't we? I know I have. And where did that get us? Why not choose the view that life is unlimited, then, and begin to experience more of that truth? You have talent. In an intelligent universe, which ours is, there is need for that talent and the opportunity to express it, or it wouldn't exist. Accept that with love, innocence, and gratitude, and then stand back and watch its fruition in your life!

2. The Principle of Infinite Resource (You Have All That You Need in the House). Good is infinite. That means—like the fast-growing vine, kudzu, in the American South—good has the run of the place! Good is the only true reality, identity,

162

presence, and power, the only everything. There is no end to it, and no existence of anything that is not good.

Wonderful, isn't it? There is no limit to good and good is everywhere. Good is expressed as you and as your thoughts and as the presence and thoughts of others. It is expressed as all desire, all business relationships, and all works of art. Good is all. To the degree that you accept it, this spiritual law will function in your life.

Again, there is much evidence that contradicts the fact that good and its resources are infinite. Nevertheless, it is a fact. And if you want more of that fact evidenced in your life and your acting career, access it by accepting it.

We always have everything that we need right within our own sphere of experience. I love that! How abundantly efficient. If we didn't, that which we seek would be out of our reach. But we do. We know someone who knows someone; we have this that will lead to that; we have it all, and we have it all right now.

Applying this principle to acting means you have the makings of a fine, talented actor, that you can expect to be given good parts to play in good productions, that you can look forward to working with good people, and that the good, receptive audiences you will be playing to—including the critics—can view your contributions and performances only as good.

3. The Principle of Absolute Dominion (Be Perfect, Even As Your Father in Heaven Is Perfect). Notice how all these truths or principles have a retinue of red-faced demons holding up demonstration signs and screaming at you, "Boy, do you have your head in the sand! Look around you, pal. Life sucks! We've got hunger, illness, poverty, and death! And you think supply meets demand?! And that good is infinite?! You think we're *perfect*? Have you seen yourself naked in the mirror lately?"

Right. I am perfect and so are you. I don't get the credit for it but yes, I am perfect. My creator, and yours, gets the credit but that doesn't make us any less perfect. I am perfect because the I that I am, is divine life, divine love, which is all good. And the more often and devotedly I claim that for myself—in spite of the evidence to the contrary—the more I will experience the presence and operation of that fact in my life.

A NOTE ABOUT DEMONSTRATION

When a defense attorney pleads a case, the first thing he does is proclaim that his client is innocent. Then he sets to work to prove his innocence. This is what we are doing when, by accepting and allowing ourselves to be ruled by spiritual principles, we claim our perfection even before we have fully demonstrated it. We say yes, we are perfect, and then, little by little, we prove it in our lives. If we don't make that seemingly premature, unsubstantiated claim, however, we have nothing to demonstrate, to prove, to *live*. There is no way to go from being guilty to being innocent, is there? Nor is there any way of living the idea, I'm not perfect, but I'm going to be. You can't get here from there. Here we are perfect. Now we are perfect. This is our authorization for also claiming that we are fine actors before we have proven in the world that we are.

4. The Principle of Complete Satisfaction (Abundantly Are You Satisfied). Abundance is the only measurement of supply. Love never runs out. Truth has no statute of limitation. Life is abundant. Forever. Life shines, it blossoms, it sings. It sings through birds and men and women. It bursts forth into beauty and richness as flowers and fruits; and it expresses itself in the forms of our abilities and talents as artists. Neither ideas nor opportunities run out, and it's never too late. Abundantly are you satisfied.

A counterreality seems to be going on. Yes, I too have seen and heard much about it. Nevertheless, the spiritual facts are true. And it is by accepting these facts that they begin to function in our lives in ways that we can appreciate and enjoy.

5. The Principle of Cause and Effect (You Reap What You Sow). Like all spiritual rules, this goes beyond the ego's interpretation of it. For instance, the ego might say, "Well, yes, everything is mental. Therefore my good or bad depends on what I thought or did, and if I'm in trouble it's because I caused it. It's my karma." No. You are entitled, and inspired, to go beyond that and say, "Yes, everything is mental, but since I, as consciousness, am good, regardless of the seeming evidence to the contrary, I neither caused nor am in any trouble at all."

Yes, you reap what you sow. But again, that doesn't mean that if you're a schmuck you reap schmuckness. It means that since you are wonderful, what you are capable of sowing can only be wonderful and so, therefore, what you reap will also be wonderful. After all, grace supersedes karma. Then, as an actor, you set out to live that. You do your armchair work. You do your preparation. You rehearse. You are thorough in sowing good, productive seeds that you may count on to produce success.

It may seem that you are working your fingers to the bone in acting but can't get a break or opportunity or a reward of any kind for your efforts. Well, this spiritual rule nullifies that apparent reality. You *reap* what you sow. Claim the fruits of your labor. By working on your art, getting your pictures out, keeping your ear to the ground to hear about upcoming roles, and doing everything else that you can, you *will* have success. Trust that. I know it flies in the face of negative truisms such as "it's who you know" or "some people have it, and some don't," but those statements are incorrect. Success is dependable; a dependable gift to those who stay at the table.

6. The Principle of Perfect Reflection (As a Man Thinks in His Heart, So Is He). Your experience is your world. By the same token, your world, the place where you live—created in large measure by what you accept as true—is your experience. "As a man thinks in his heart" means what he accepts as true. You are not at the mercy of events, economic conditions, or the whims of other people. Nor in the long run are you even at the mercy of what *you* accept as true unless it *is* true; because unless it is true, you will eventually see through it. And the sooner you accept the veracity of these spiritual principles, the sooner you will have the experience of their veracity in your life.

Again, your experience is your world—or, at the least, your world of experience. It is mental, spiritual, and subjective—not objective or outside yourself. We all partake of the overall Earth curriculum, but your experience of it is subjective and, in large degree, subject only to you. Your acting career, therefore, is not at the mercy of anything outside yourself. It seems like it is subject to competition, the in-crowd, limited resources, and pilot season. But it isn't. It is dependent on your power to accept the truth about it. The good news is that because we do have the mind of God, we do believe in good. Therefore that is what we, inevitably, eventually experience.

7. The Principle of Ongoing Progress (Progress Is the Law). This too is a fact of all life. We progress. Everyday everything progresses. Precept upon precept. Line upon line. Here a little, there a little. We can trust that *our* progress, too, is certain; our success is assured.

It may sometimes look like we're standing still or going backward. But life is not static and it doesn't go backward. If it seems like we're going backward, that means that we weren't as far ahead as we thought we were. "I'm slipping backward!" No, you're not, you just weren't on solid ground before, and you're now waking up to that fact—which is progress.

There is so much to this wonderful life that we live. Although there is much that we do control, there is so much more that we don't. So we might just as well relax and let life live *us*. We can go kicking and screaming—full of doubt and fear— or we can catch on to the fact that a ride as magnificent as this one is must have some intelligent inner workings and go along and enjoy the ride. It's life's job to make sure that each one of its children does it proud, reaches the goal post, crosses the finish line—not that there is a finish line, since life is eternal. The point is, you can relax about your acting career. As long as you are giving it attention and focus every day, you cannot fail to progress.

8. The Law of Reciprocity (The Law of Mutual Exchange or Give and Take). Reciprocity is defined as "mutual dependence, action, or influence; mutual exchange; a mutual recognition by each of two parties of the validity, privileges, and value of the other."

Reciprocity. The word feels good rolling off the tongue, doesn't it? In acting, it means mutual honor and appreciation between actor and director, actor and producer, actor and actor, and actor and audience. It means I am recognized as a valuable player by you, and you are recognized as a valuable player by me. It excludes either the tendency to look down one's nose or up from the ground at another. It means the universal respect, appreciation, and love that life has for each of its manifestations, as well as that which each manifestation has for every other.

9. The Law of Recompense (The Laborer Is Worthy of His Hire). Recompense is balanced compensation, an equivalent for something done or given.

You can depend on making a good living for your contributions to society throughout your acting career because life itself is our ever-conscious employer. Therefore, by the law of recompense, our slightest effort is appreciated and abundantly compensated. Our slightest effort away from the beliefs of fear and limitation is rewarded by relief, inspiration, and joy. Our slightest effort to shine, to grow, to improve our conditions, and to develop our talents is rewarded with success. Conscious Love is pleased with you, proud of you; she shows her approbation by answering your prayers, fulfilling your dreams, and satisfying your every desire. This is a good employer, wouldn't you say? Life is a job with *benefits*! Please be clear about something else as well. You don't work for a living. You work to express yourself, to grow, and for the joy of working. Nor does success come from making money; money comes from success. You do the work, yes, but God is the prospering principle and provides your living in recompense for your faithfully following your heart.

10. The Law of Luck (By Grace You Are Saved). I met a woman who, when I told her I was looking for an apartment in New York City, said, "Good luck, because you need luck." Let's discuss this idea of luck. If you truly do need luck, then, by the principle of the coincidence of supply and demand, you must already have it.

Some people say luck is the residue of effort; others say luck is when preparedness meets opportunity. But that's not what we mean when we wish someone good luck or say "Boy, is she lucky!" The residue of effort pertains more to the law that you reap what you sow; and preparedness meets opportunity describes the process of progress. It is wonderful that opportunities do come, and it's cool to be ready for them when they do, but here we're talking about the reward of hard work, not luck. Somebody on a lucky streak is a person who is the recipient of things that were *not* the residue of his effort; it was not the result of his doing anything. It was a gift. It was *grace* if you want to use the religious term. It was luck.

Not many people consider luck a law—spiritual or otherwise. If anything, they consider it superstitious to believe in luck. That's because most people mistakenly believe that luck is selective, a matter of chance. Some people have all the luck, they say in the same way that they say some people have talent and some don't. But that's where the problem lies. Success is the birthright of us all. There is no predestination, preselection, or chance to it. Good—well-being—is given to each of us. Luck means that when I ask—I don't even *have* to ask—"May I have something just because I desire it, *not* because I earned it or deserve it?" the answer is "Absolutely," because life is good. That's what makes us lucky—the wonderful miracle that life is good. The woman I met was right. We do need luck because we can't do it all ourselves. And because we need it to succeed, it is already supplied in the consciousness of each of us. We have it. It's part of our equipment. No chance. No favorites. No exceptions. Life is absolutely mad about all of us. So it's not superstitious to claim that you are lucky, it's spiritual. Because you are doing so as a wonder-struck child whose prayer might be, "Thank you, dear life, for your great generosity. You have kept your promise—you have given me the kingdom. Boy, oh boy, am I lucky."

That's what I did. I accessed my luck by subscribing to it. And two days later I found the adorable—and rent-stabilized—apartment I was looking for. But then, of course, *I* was lucky!

11. The Principle of the Fulfillment of True Desire (Ask and You Shall Receive: You Get What You Really Want). Desire is destiny. It is a psychic diamond that points to your future because that's where you are headed. Now, you can go kicking and screaming and claim you didn't mean it, you didn't really want to go where you are headed, and allow fear, doubt, and other forms of resistance to delay the trip; or you can take responsibility and honor your desires and the unthwartable efficacy of them, and follow them to their, and *your,* ultimate fulfillment. A tip? Go the latter route. It's faster and less painful.

You can depend on life to hold your hand and escort you along your chosen path of acting. In fact, if you will refrain from sabotaging yourself and go along with your own dreams, you'll find that you will have to hurry to keep up with them! And why not? You get to be *happy;* you get to have what you *really* want. Because it is by following your true desires that

169

you best learn the lessons that life has to teach you—for we do live in a perfect universe.

12. The Principle of Universal Success (Not One of Them Shall Be Lost). This principle has a special place in my heart. By the principle of universal success, you are on a free ride! You can relax. No problem. No sweat. No worry. For the universe as a whole to succeed—to be fully what it is capable of being— every element of it must be successful. So it's a done deal! Our success is inevitable. It's guaranteed because life needs and causes us to be successful so that it, overall, succeeds. This is perfection at its grandest. The way that pertains to your acting I am sure you can figure out on your own. Suffice it to say, you can chill and enjoy the ride!

THE BOTTOM LINE

The bottom line on a business organization's quarterly financial statement shows how much money the business made that quarter. The bottom line in life, though, when you look at profit from a spiritual standpoint, takes on a different meaning. It means how much good did you create in your life and your world this quarter? How much of a positive difference did you make? That's what we really want to do with our acting, don't we? We want to make a positive impact on this world while we are here on pilgrimage. That is the bottom line.

THE SYSTEM

Sometimes I think of God, or life, as *the system*, the big pot that includes everything, the whole kit and caboodle. And there's only one *whole* anything, isn't there? The same way that we think of the body as the overall physical system, I think of life, or God, as the one perfectly functioning spiritual system.

There is only one overall system, therefore, to which we are subject. And it is not the Hollywood system or some teacher's acting system or even some economic system. On the contrary, Hollywood and Broadway and Timbuktu, and everyone in them, as well as all our systems of acting and the economy and everything else, are all subject to the one real system that governs all—the living reality we call God. That is the only system you and your acting career are subject to and none other. So, there is no *chance* that you *might* make it as an actor but, then again, *might not;* there is certainty to this system, which functions according to dependable, spiritual principles.

There is room for all of us. There must be; we're all here. There's room and there's opportunity. It does not require magic to make it in acting. It requires dedication, learning your craft, learning the ropes, hard work, faith, and a little grace from on high—like it does in every other enterprise—but no magic. Regardless of the evidence to the contrary—which can be mind-boggling at times—we all exist in the one perfect system of spirit, and we can all trust that our success is assured.

⊛ *Affirmation*

I live according to the spiritual laws of being and, therefore, I am secure, successful, and satisfied.

※ EXERCISE

For each of the spiritual principles listed below, please write down a circumstance to which you believe (or can imagine) applying the principle would further your acting career.

1. By applying the Principle of the Coincidence of Supply and Demand

_____

_____

_____.

2. By applying the Principle of Infinite Resource

_____

_____

_____.

3. By applying the Principle of Absolute Dominion

_____

_____

_____.

4. By applying the Principle of Complete Satisfaction

_____

_____

_____.

5. By applying the Principle of Cause and Effect

_____

_____

_____.

6. By applying the Principle of Perfect Reflection

_____

_____

_____.

7. By applying the Principle of Ongoing Progress

_____

_____

_____.

8. By applying the Law of Reciprocity

_____

_____

_____ .

9. By applying the Law of Recompense

_____

_____

_____ .

10. By applying the Law of Luck

_____

_____

_____ .

11. By applying the Principle of the Fulfillment
of True Desire

_____

_____

_____ .

12. By applying the Principle of Universal Success

_____

_____

_____ .

SUMMARY OF MAIN POINTS

1. The only reason to break rules is if they limit or abuse you; then you are not truly bound by them.
2. There exist spiritual principles or laws, however, that are unbreakable rules because they are life-supporting. These are the spiritual rules or principles by which the game of life is played.

3. Some of the spiritual principles by which we play the game of life are:

> The principle of the coincidence of supply and demand
> The principle of infinite resource
> The principle of absolute dominion
> The principle of complete satisfaction
> The principle of cause and effect
> The principle of perfect reflection
> The principle of ongoing progress
> The law of reciprocity
> The law of recompense
> The law of luck
> The principle of the fulfillment of true desire
> The principle of universal success

4. There is only one system to which we and our businesses are subject: life itself.

5. There is no chance in the system of life; within it spiritual principles continually and unfalteringly operate.

6. There is room and opportunity for all of us to succeed. Much is required of us, but we can trust that under the one perfect system of spirit, our success is assured.

CHAPTER 18

Opportunities

Soul has infinite resources with which to bless mankind.

—Mary Baker Eddy

Opportunities are like oranges. They do grow on trees. They are everywhere around you. You will never have to hope that opportunities will occur, because they never fail to exist; nor do they exist outside yourself. You are in the fortunate position of being provided with—and, in fact, are in possession of—more opportunities than you will ever be able to use. It is up to you, at your own time in your own way, to choose the ones that seem most attractive to you. And you can trust that you will be inspired to choose the ones that will most promote your growth.

Like fruit on a tree, the more you pick the greater the crop next season. But you can't use them all, nor need you. Some opportunities will fall on the ground. That's all right. Let them. The ones that are right for you, you will be led to select even if it seems to take you a long time to become ready to do so. In fact, opportunities only become functional when they *are* selected and used. So you can't really blow opportunities. And

175

the ones that fall on the ground will seed the ground and create more opportunities in the future because good is eternally fertile and productive.

Eventually, you will feel brave enough to pluck one from a tree. Or, if you, at least, remain on the field, one may just land on your head. Something will tell you an opportunity is for you and encourage you to accept it. Do so. Trust that the opportunities that come are right for you—no matter how grand or modest they seem. Be willing to take life one baby step at a time. If your ambition is to be a film actor and you are offered a commercial, take it, as long as you can promote the product in good conscience because you can see that it is helpful to your brothers and sisters. If you are offered a part on a soap opera, don't refuse because you want to do theater. Take it. Trust that every event in your career is governed by divine intelligence. These first opportunities come to prepare you. Remember, your journey is process, not goal, oriented. And within the process, your art and your career unfold step by step to reach their apotheosis. If you're not yet ready for an opportunity and you pass on it, that's fine. That means it wasn't really *your* opportunity. If it had been, you would have taken it. It will come around again. And maybe the next time you won't turn it down.

BE PERFORMANCE-READY

Become performance-ready. Be ready for these opportunities when they come. You are an actor. Therefore, you are going to get opportunities to act. You must become ready to use those opportunities.

Many artists I know are hung up by the belief that if they don't have an audience, they can't perform their art. If he doesn't have a record deal, he can't be a singer. If she doesn't have a book contract, she can't be a writer. If they are not starring in a play, they can't be actors. That is not true, even for an actor, whose performance seems group-dependent. An actor can act all by herself in her armchair. After all, most of the work that you do *is* done in your armchair in your preparation work. The point is, do your preparation work so you are ready when your opportunities come.

How many times have you been asked to perform and because you didn't feel ready, said no? How many bands have you been asked to join? How many productions have you been asked to be part of? How often have you been asked to sing or recite, but fear, inhibition, or insecurity prevented you, largely because you didn't feel you were ready? You couldn't think of a poem or monologue or song on the spot, and so the opportunity passed you by. They make for sad stories, those wounded moments, don't they? We all have at least one of them. They're nothing to feel ashamed of or despondent about because they're part of growing, but we don't have to have any more of them.

Get a monologue or two, a serious one and a comedic one. Break them down. Figure out what each is about. Learn them. Then learn a couple of poems and a couple of songs. Do it. Become ready to perform when somebody asks you to. The opportunities do come. And you want to be ready to step up to bat, so you can feel you are playing—and having a blast!—in the kingdom.

EXERCISE

Write an ode to one of your favorite historical figures, memorize it, then perform it.

ALWAYS PERFORM WHEN ASKED

During our introductory interview, I always ask my prospective students to make an agreement with me before I take them on to study. "Will you agree," I ask, "that, from this moment on, you will always perform when you are asked to? If you are at a party and someone asks you to give a monologue, will you do it? If someone asks you to recite a poem or sing a song, will you do it, instead of saying, 'Oh, no, I couldn't,' and shyly slinking away?" I request—I require, in fact—that my students make this agreement because it is crucial to their success.

If you are not willing to make this agreement, then you are not ready to work. You have to be willing to perform to the best of your ability *now*. You improve in your work as you practice it, and because performance work is performed in front of people, you grow in performance work as you perform in front of people. This only makes sense, right? You must be willing to suffer the growing pains (including embarrasment) that goes along with growing. You have to be willing to do what is asked of you or you will never get past the fear. You have to be willing to make a fool of yourself and to fail. But it is only by this willingness, which comes more and more easily once you have experienced that you can survive failure, that you will conquer that fear and grow.

To most effectively—and most comfortably—accept each opportunity to perform, you must be performance-ready. I suggest that you have at your fingertips two monologues, two songs, and two poems, which you have selected because they embrace ideas and sentiments that you believe in.

EXERCISE

Assemble six sheets of paper. Title the first, Monologue 1; the second, Monologue 2; the third, Song 1; the fourth, Song 2; the fifth, Poem 1, and the sixth, Poem 2. Then check your mental files. Do you already have one or two of them selected, a comedic monologue you love, for instance, or a song or poem? Good. Write or type out the words on the appropriate sheet. You are becoming performance-ready. While you are searching for the others, learn the pieces that you have.

ACTORS MUST ASSERT THEMSELVES

Opportunities may, and often do, come via invitations from others. But many more times they occur only through your own self-assertion. You may be at a party, for instance. Three or four actors get up and each does his or her thing, and yet nobody asks you to do yours. It is then, at such times—and they happen often—that you have to muster your courage and say, "My turn! I have a monologue that I'd like to do, if I may." If your hostess replies, "No, thanks. The fondue is finally bubbling," then so be it. You've done your part in your developmental process as an artist by having come forth with courage and willingness. Ninety-nine percent of the time she will not, however. She will say, "Sure. Let's have it!" And you will exercise your performance-readiness. And afterward you will feel delighted with yourself that you did.

One reason actors have to self-assert is that the egos of others often keep them from inviting other people to perform. But, by universal law, each one of us is self-governed. So, it's really not up to *them* to give you your opportunities, anyway. Opportunities will come *through* others at times, of course, but even then they will usually be coming via the self-interest of others. And that's all right, too. If someone is directing a play, for instance, he will need actors to be in it. It's his need that creates the opportunity for you. And he may then midwife your opportunity, but not as a favor to you, which is how it should be. It keeps everybody in the game. But you can't depend on your opportunities coming through others. Nor should you spend any time resenting the fact that you can't. It would be very nice if Prince Charming would come along in the form of Martin Scorsese and say, "It's you! I've finally found you! I'm going to make you a movie star!" and sweep you off your feet into absolute star-studded wonderfulness, but that is not the way that it works. OK, it may have worked that way *once*. We've all heard the story of Lana Turner's being discovered at Schwab's

Drug Store. But have you ever heard of anyone else being discovered there? That sort of thing happens so infrequently, in fact, that it's not worth spending any time hoping that it will happen to you. And that's not being negative. The truth is, most of the time we have to get up and get it ourselves. And that's fine!

⊛ *Affirmation*

> *We are all stars, and life needs us all to shine for life to be fully aglitter. I am a star!*

So get on with it. Assert yourself. After all, that's how we grow. Don't wait and hope for a big break to come. Breaks will come, but they usually don't come in big sizes, and they result from the oranges *you* pick—each one leading to the next. Your job, which facilitates the progressive utilization of those breaks, is to stay on your path, take your everyday steps, and not be afraid to assert yourself.

※ EXERCISE

Practice and improve your cold-reading skills, first by yourself and then with a scene partner. Keep your skills up to par so you are ready when your opportunities come.

HE WHO HESITATES . . .

Why don't we assert ourselves? The obvious reason is that we're afraid that we can't deliver, that we'll blow it. But there's another reason. We're afraid that we will be considered too pushy. After all, we have been taught to be humble.

Humility is a good thing, but to be humble does not mean believing that we are chopped liver. To be humble is to understand that we are the evidence of all that is glorious; and it is humble to demonstrate that fact by utilizing the opportunities that come to us. We do not wait. We refuse to be imprisoned in that girl space at the dance where we wait to be asked, to be *chosen.* No. We walk right out onto the dance floor ourselves and, with or without a partner, we dance. Then afterward, we walk up to the table and fill our own plate from the abundant cornucopia. We need neither the permission nor the approval from anyone else to be fully who we are. There is enough for everyone; but you have to go get it yourself.

Women, more than men, are slammed for asserting themselves. We've all heard the criticism of Barbra Streisand, for instance: boy, is she a pushy broad, and so on. But assertive women *and* men are slammed by people who are blocked in their own self-expression. People who are afraid that *they* can't do it, that they don't have what it takes, that there's not enough for them—they're the ones who slam those of us who, often through blood, sweat, and tears, have fought those very demons ourselves and are taking a stand that we *can,* we *do,* and there *is!* They don't realize that those of us who muster enough courage to assert ourselves do so because we, like them, have the natural impulse to do so, which causes us to prosper; more— to survive! They think it would be nicer if we just sat still and died.

To hell with that, campers! We're not here to be nice. We're here to love, yes, but we have to love ourselves first. Lucille Ball said, "Love yourself first and everything else falls into line." For if we fail to love ourselves, what have we to offer to the world? Cultivate self-assertion. You may be called a bit pushy and spoken of as a little bit aggressive, but people will admire you for it and add, "I guess that's what it takes to get it done." And they will be right.

HAVE FUN

Have fun in the work. That's an order! We're talking about joyful participation in the action. Enjoy determining and expressing emotion for the purpose of revealing truth. Know that your take is intelligent, worthy, and good and that it must be appreciated as good by others because there truly is only one mind. And don't worry. No matter how many opportunities you think you have blown, as long as you exist—which, as it happens, will be forever—there will always be more opportunities. You will never run out, and it will never be too late, because it is an inevitable function of your nature to fulfill your potential. Trust in the love and generosity of life that sees to it that all of her children succeed. To put all of this into practice, agree to:

1. Become performance-ready
2. Perform when asked
3. Assert yourself
4. Enjoy and trust the process

NOW JUMP IN!

Get involved. Don't wait; do it now. Find out what projects are being done. Producers print notices of their productions in trade papers such as *The Hollywood Reporter*, *Variety*, and *Backstage*. Try to audition for them as an actor, but if the production is already cast or they don't have a part for you, find another way to get in on the project to gain experience. There are plenty of ways you can work. You just have to be creative about finding them. Make the decision that you want to work, and oranges will start falling on your head.

Then take it further if you want to. Direct, produce, and/or star in your own play or film. People with no more smarts or talent or money than you have do it all the time. It doesn't have to be an expensive undertaking. You may not make your money back on your first one—but that may be all right, if you consciously make that decision. Other rewards, such as further opportunities or getting a good agent, may make that worth it to you. The point is, there is plenty that you can do.

"Ah, it'll never work!" Has this nasty little thought occured to you? Of course. Is it true? No! Doing your spiritual work, as well as the work on your craft, *is* the work, and that work inevitably progresses. It may take a while—it *will* take a while—but if you do nothing but wait for a good part, a good opportunity, or for someone else to hand it to you, you may end up waiting a very long time.

※ EXERCISE

Select 1 Corinthians, Chapter 13; Proverbs, Chapter 31; Psalm 23; or Psalm 91; break it down, memorize, and perform it.

GOD IS THE PROSPERING PRINCIPLE

Remember, God is the prospering principle and work is for the purpose of self-expression—the development and expression of our God-given faculties and powers—so that we do our part in contributing to the ongoing magnificence that is life. But it is life itself that provides both the opportunities and the compensation for our doing that. After all, it is through us that divine intelligence expresses itself. And when our motive to blossom and serve is in place, we know we are entitled to success and doubt vanishes.

MEANING IT

In acting, more than in any other profession, you get experience in meaning it, in *meaning* what you say and do. You practice *meaning it* with every word of dialogue that you utter. You have to; the only way the audience will buy what you are saying is if *you* mean it. When you say to yourself that your success is assured, be sure that you understand and mean that, too. Don't just say the words.

We have so much to be grateful for. We are the characters in God's play, created, constituted, and governed by the great Author who sees us all as happy, healthy, and successful. Let's relax and play our parts in this. Allow your present condition, whatever it is, to be a fully functioning opportunity for you to demonstrate your success.

✹ EXERCISE

List twenty things you are grateful for—from the mundane to the sublime—then write a short three-verse poem that uses every entry on your list. Memorize it and perform it.

SUMMARY OF MAIN POINTS

1. You possess more opportunities than you will ever be able to use. You can trust life to inspire you to choose the ones that will best promote your growth.
2. Good is infinitely and eternally fertile and productive.
3. Opportunities become functional only when they are used.
4. It will never be too late. There is one time in reality, and that time is now and always.
5. Do not refuse opportunities because they appear modest. Modest opportunities prepare you for bigger ones.
6. Become performance-ready.

7. Always perform when asked. You improve as you practice, and because performance work is done in front of others, you grow as you practice performing in front of people.

8. Actors must self-assert. Don't wait and hope for an invitation or a break. They will come, but your job, and that which facilitates the best use of those invitations and breaks, is to take your everyday steps.

9. It is an inevitable function of your nature to fulfill its potential; so you can relax and enjoy the ride!

10. Opportunities occur to facilitate your inevitable self-expression.

11. Make the decision that you are willing to work, and oranges will start falling on your head.

12. We don't work to make an income; we work to develop and express our talents. God is the prospering principle upon which we can depend to prosper and compensate us for our efforts.

CHAPTER 19

Debunking
Scarcity Statistics

*I merely took the energy it takes to pout and wrote
some blues.*

—Duke Ellington

I've made a lot of positive statements in this book; yet all we
have to do is turn on the television to hear that the cold season is upon us, a tornado wreaked havoc in Mexico, and the
stock market has crashed. Regardless of your willingness to
think positive, says this point of view, things are not looking
so good.

This is not news to us, however. We're used to it. We're barraged by the fearful claims that good is ridiculous and evil is
the true reality. I recently saw a film, for instance, that promotes
the belief that contagion is real, unavoidable, and deadly. You
have no chance, it says; you are subject to a variety of deadly
diseases and you are powerless to fight them off. In other words,
you're a goner. That's the message of the film: life sucks. That
is art at its lowest—but that's another conversation.

The only chance we have of combating this flow of negativity and achieving anything close to a happy life is by doing our daily spiritual work as mental warriors in the fight against this godless baloney. Actors have to monitor their thinking to meet these negative thoughts, these opponents that try to defeat them before they ever get out on the field.

YOU HAVE NO LIMITATIONS

What are the faces of the opponents on our playing field? How do we recognize these would-be limiters that we hear around us? They are the ones who tell us we have too much or too little of something we need to succeed. We're too old, too fat, too poor, or too late; we're not tough enough; we don't have a good enough agent, enough contacts, or enough hair. In short, we are not what they're looking for.

None of us is perfect according to the standards the above criticisms allude to. Nevertheless, it's impossible to have too little of anything because you are complete. Furthermore, since you are in the sandbox, you are already a player, a player who represents a large contingent of other human beings like yourself. And you have the same consciousness in common with *every*one else. You are a perfect candidate to be a successful working actor.

The criticisms, accusations, and judgments must be ruthlessly dismissed from your consciousness. They are the enemy. You have no limitations. You have 100 percent current value, now and forever. You possess, to an ever-increasing degree, the experiential understanding of the human condition as well as the willingness to represent that on stage. That is all you need as an actor.

ACTING IS NOT GAMBLING

Besides the limiters in their corner, another coterie of opponents stands in another corner on the field under their banner, "The Odds Against Making It." Not *for*, mind you, but *against*. That should be warning enough against your heeding it. "Do you have any idea what the odds against your making it as an actor are?!" they say, as if they are the great realists.

We think of odds in gambling, don't we? Well, we are not in Las Vegas, nor do its game rules apply to us. We are in heaven. We are neither dealing with, nor concerned about, what somebody *else* has come up with as the so-called odds against *our* making it. We are not dealing with chance. We are dealing with principled, spiritual certainties, which are worthy of our trust in their promises.

Take a look at some of those scary Screen Actors Guild statistics, one might counter. Do you know how few actors really make it in this business? Do you know how few actors make even a modest living in this business? Yes, we know. But we also know that life is a subjective experience, and that our experience of life is determined by *our* vision of it, not that of others. Knowing this, we place ourselves under a more dependable source of provision.

IT'S WHO YOU ARE, NOT WHO YOU KNOW

In a third corner of the playing field is another group of opponents sniveling and bumping into one another under their banner that reads "It's Who You Know." Wrong. These jerks say that if your mother doesn't run a studio and your cousin— or somebody who screwed somebody *known* by your cousin— isn't a big agent at William Morris, then you may as well give up because you don't have a . . . a what? A *chance*. But we're not looking for chances. We're looking for definite steps of progress.

It's not who you know. You could be the biggest schmuck in the world and know everybody, and it's not going to do you one bit of good. It's who you *are*. Who you are determines what you do, which people will see and judge you by and which will make them want to work with you, because they will see your value. Who you *are* is everything.

THE CLIMATE *INSIDE* MATTERS

And in the final corner of our field stands another potentially harmful band of agitators. The banner above their heads reads "It's the Business Climate That Matters." Wrong again! It is not the climate outside, but the climate inside that matters. In fact, nothing that truly has anything to do with you *is* going on outside of yourself because life is subjective. Your experience of the world mirrors your thoughts and feelings the same way that, on stage, your character's words and actions mirror his thoughts and feelings. Right in the middle of pilot season or a union strike, some actors secure agents. In the depth of an economic depression, some people thrive. Right in the midst of a cattle call, some actresses make the cut. Why? Because they didn't succumb to the picture of "the impossible" as others did.

Every time you hear a statistic of scarcity, mentally combat it. Pull the rug out from under it. Laugh at it. Say no. Instead, make a claim for the good. Then you will not fall subject to it. Stay on your toes, though, because the little demons never sleep. They remain ready to attack you until you have thoroughly destroyed them.

BE WILLING TO BE IN THE FIGHT

Adopt the attitude of a willing warrior, a dependable worker in the workshop, a valuable player on the field. Agree to fight, to work, and to play. Get on the field, stay on the field, and *play hard*. Don't give up; be in it for the long haul. Be there. Show up every day. Tell fear and all its scarcity statistics to take their best shots. *You* know that you are invincible, because you are a player, a hard worker, a warrior for good; for you, nothing can prove seriously daunting.

Remember that the human experience, including its career occupations, is a spiritual pilgrimage whose purpose is for us to demonstrate our dominion over all limiting mental concepts. Every seed has within itself the impulse to grow, which sustains it in the darkness until it breaks through the earth to meet the sunlight. So it is with you. Your career, your experience, your life is a partnership with God. You and God are partners. So, who's to fail? The partnership of "God and You" is invincible. Yes, God *and* you. Because, as with the plant, even the great sun itself would have no power were it not for the impulse to grow that resides within the soul of the seed.

Our fight is with mental concepts, however, not with "reality," and certainly not with each other. It is a tragic illusion that suggests the fight is with one another, that it's a dog-eat-dog world, that people are out after only their own good, that we have to get *ours* before someone else does, that there is only so much (so *little*) to go around, and that the competition is fierce. Refuse to fight your brother or sister. Realize that doing so would merely disrupt your own progress. We are together, all of us, fighting the same fight, the same concepts of limitation. Let us fight together. Let us love and refuse to believe that the enemy is one another instead of the fear that would mesmerize all of us. We are on a mission, and reality, which includes every spiritual principle and all of our brothers and sisters, is on our side. We are on a mission that will succeed, fighting a fight we will win, playing a game we will ace, because it is life—love—that is living us and will ultimately secure the outcome of the battle. And good acting in a good play illustrates that glorious fact.

190

EVERY TYPE IS NEEDED

Every type of actor is needed. *You* are needed. And again, it is never too late. If you are 116 years old and look like a prune but still have the impulse to act, we need you! We need you and we have work for you. When you accept that for yourself, the opportunities will become apparent because by accepting these truths you initiate the events that illustrate them in your experience.

YOU ARE THE ONLY THINKER IN YOUR UNIVERSE

Only the way *you* think determines your experience. Isn't that wonderful? This is power. It's God-given—it didn't derive from you—but it is your power to live for the good. You are not subject to limitations, chances, or the so-called vagaries of life. You have chosen to be an actor because that is the right way for you to develop and express your individuality. You know that, and you are inevitably destined to succeed.

✺ *Affirmation*

I am the only thinker in my universe.

COMPETITION

It's fine to say we all get to be successful and that there are no limits, but isn't there a limited number of parts? And don't actors have to compete for them?

Competition, as a spiritual concept, exists to help each participant bring out the best in him- or herself. That is its only function. We don't beat one another out. On the contrary, we make sure everybody gets in. So when you hear there is a part you believe you are right for, you are correct—you *are* right for

191

the part. Ten other actors competing with you may be right for it too. Your task is to do your work fully; that means, play to win and trust that the powers that be—that reside within you *and* your competitors—will see to it that you, and they, win enough parts to give you all satisfying, lucrative careers.

You are a star! You are meant to shine! Do not dull your own brilliance by accepting the fearful beliefs of scarcity and think "Chances are I won't get this part," as you walk in the door to audition. "Be alert," as a bookmark I was once given said, "for the world needs all the lerts it can get!"

✻ EXERCISE

List five little demons that plague you, that say your success is unlikely (such as you are too _____, or not enough _____), and then state the truth, or spiritual antidote, that destroys them.

1. I am _____.
   However, that is not really true because
   _____.

2. I am _____.
   However, that is not really true because
   _____.

3. Life is _____.
   However, that is not really true because
   _____.

4. It seems like _____.
   However, that is not really true because
   _____.

5. I am _____.
   However, that is not really true because
   _____.

❂ *Affirmation*

I have what it takes, it is never too late; my success is presently occurring.

SUMMARY OF MAIN POINTS

1. We are barraged daily by messages of limitation; the only way we can effectively combat them is to do our daily spiritual work.
2. You are in the sandbox *now;* therefore, you have already been selected to be a successful player.
3. Criticisms, accusations, judgments, and all other limitations must be summarily dismissed from the consciousness of the aspiring actor. Those limiters are the faces of the enemy.
4. Regarding making it in acting, the notion of odds or chances does not enter into our consideration. We are relying on a higher source of opportunity and provision. We are dealing with certainties.
5. It is not who you know; it's who you are.
6. The spiritual climate in business is always favorable.
7. Be a willing and diligent mental warrior against all mental opponents and realize that you are never fighting or competing with your brothers or sisters. On the contrary, you and your brothers and sisters are all fighting together against so-called limitations—the fodder by which you, ultimately, prove your mettle.
8. You are the only thinker in your universe. So, stay alert!

CHAPTER 20

Representation

As artists, we must find those who believe in us, and in whom we believe, and band together for support, encouragement, and protection.

— Julia Cameron

FINDING THE RIGHT REPRESENTATION

OK, now let's talk about representation. Not only do *you* represent a state of mind each time you play a character, but the business of acting is set up in such a way that the actor himself needs representation as he forges forward in the business of his career. How do you find that representation? The four most often asked questions regarding representation are:

1. Do I need an agent?
2. How do I find an agent?
3. Do I need both an agent and a manager?
4. Can I represent and submit myself for auditions?

John Cusak was recently quoted as saying, "To make it as a successful actor in this business, you have to be a leader." I agree. You are the boss—it's your career—so you need to lead.

But, yes, you also need an agent if you want to get the calls that bring in the real money in this business.

✖ EXERCISE

Be twelve years old again and answer the question, What do you want to be when you grow up?

_____

_____

THE BREAKDOWNS

The way the business has developed, most calls for auditions today are transmitted via a fax machine or computer by an organization called Breakdown Services, Ltd. The transmissions themselves are called "the breakdowns." Each breakdown lists a production that is casting and describes the characters the production company is casting for, including each character's physical type and main action. These breakdowns are transmitted to licensed Screen Actors Guild–affiliated agents, personal managers, and other subscribers, mostly through Internet websites. All subscribers first sign a confidentiality agreement. It is illegal to get the breakdowns from any other source than Breakdown Services; the information is copyrighted.

Since this service is geared for agents, individual actors are not permitted to subscribe to the service. Some actors do get the breakdowns illegally, however, and often share them. And some agents allow their acting clients to come and take a look at the breakdowns and recommend themselves for submission. But the prescribed way of using the breakdowns is that the SAG-affiliated agent subscribes to the service, reviews the breakdowns, selects from his stable of actors those actors whom he thinks fits the breakdown, pulls the pictures and résumés of those actors, and sends them via messenger in an envelope to the casting director who posted the breakdowns for that particular show. The casting director then looks at the pictures and decides whether or not he wants to call any of the submitted actors in for an audition. If so, he then calls the agent and sets up a time, and the agent then calls the actor.

That, in a nutshell, is the way it's done. Therefore, to get in on a call, especially a call that offers money, you do need to have a SAG-affiliated agent. Furthermore, because this business is so fraught with deadlines, casting directors often don't even review pictures submitted by smaller agencies unless they can't find what they are looking for from the midsize or bigger ones. This is sad news for the beginning actor; it's another hurdle to clear on the playing field. But it is also another prompt to seek a good agent, and the actor is better off when he is aware of it.

FINDING AN AGENT

So yes, you do need to find a good agent, and you need to begin the process of finding one (two, if you also want a commercial agent) now. Go to Samuel French Bookstore in Hollywood or New York, or Drama Book Shop or Applause in New York, or another bookstore that caters to showbiz—or call any of these bookstores and deal with them by phone and mail—and buy a book that lists the current SAG-affiliated agencies. Acting World Books publishes one called *The Agencies*—both a New York and a Los Angeles edition and both editions are updated every month. K. Callan puts out two good books of agents, one for New York, one for Los Angeles. *The Ross Reports*, published monthly, lists New York agents, casting directors, and other information. Henderson Publications in New York publishes packages of mailing labels for agents, as well as for casting directors and others. Or you can call Screen Actors Guild, and for a nominal charge they will send you a list of SAG-affiliated agencies.

CULLING YOUR LIST OF AGENTS

There are different ways of sending your mailings to agents. Some actors do a mass mailing to every agent in every agency in every book. I don't think that is efficient. It's a huge, expensive undertaking and the A+ you get for thoroughness can be knocked down to an F because you may end up with an agent who, in your heart of hearts, you didn't really want in the first place. I suggest you go at it differently.

Use one good list, either one you buy off the shelf or one you compile. The current issue of the Los Angeles edition of *The Agencies*, for instance, lists approximately 250 agencies. Let's say you live in Los Angeles and you decide to use that list. First go through it and determine which agents specifically are *not* for you, such as those that represent particular categories that you don't fit into by race, age, skill, etc. That may leave you with a list of about 200.

Next, go through the list again and eliminate those that say "never any new people." The bigger agencies, such as William Morris, ICM, and CAA—the large packaging agencies—have their hands full with star actors, writers, producers, and directors. The likelihood of one them deciding to represent the not-quite-yet-rising star is so minimal it's not even worth going for it. I know there are exceptions, but I recommend that you look for listings that are more receptive to new talent.

If a listing says "occasionally new talent," those agencies are worth taking a look at because that door, while not wide open, is at least open. Better yet, go for a midlist or smaller agent who needs you as much as you need him or her, who will spend time with you, who will be glad, even excited, to have you on his or her roster. You'll secure an agent in a shorter period of time that way and, therefore, you'll get out on auditions sooner. In the same way that you follow the Tao of acting by finding the roles that you can most naturally play, go also with the Tao of finding an agent.

Once you've got your list culled to a 100 agents or so (if in Los Angeles) or around sixty (if in New York), you are ready to solicit your representation. And that you will do through the mail; generally speaking, none of the agents on your list is receptive to walk-ins. That doesn't mean *you* shouldn't walk in. It's your life and career—do it your way. But agents don't encourage it. Mailing your submissions is the accepted way. Here are a couple of ways to do that:

1. Narrow down your list to between twenty-five and fifty of what seem to be the best agents, any one of which you would be delighted to have; send your submissions (head shot, résumé, and cover letter) to all of them at the same time and wait a month. If you don't get a response, send to them all again. If you don't get a response, send to them all a third time. If you don't hear anything after three submissions to the same people, then send to either different agents at the same agencies or to agents at new agencies, applying the same procedure.

2. Here's another way. Send your submissions to the first twenty on your list. Wait two weeks. If you haven't heard from any of them, send out to the next twenty. Wait two weeks. If you get no response, send out to the next twenty—and so on until you have made it through your list. If you have made it through but haven't heard from any of them, start over again.

These are suggestions; you may come up with others. But don't be discouraged if it takes three or four or six months to get a response. It probably will. Advertising experts tell us it usually takes at least three points of introduction to a new product before a consumer begins to feel comfortable enough with it to try it. This process takes time. Be your own trusty secretary and, with little emotional investment in it, handle each mailing as a simple task. Put it on your calendar. On the fifteenth, or the tenth, or the first of every month, compile and send out your mailings until you are called in for an interview by an agent. And don't worry; you will be. You are fabulous!

❋ EXERCISE

Put an agents mailing list together. Include only those agents you would really like to represent you.

ADDRESSING YOUR SUBMISSIONS

Address your envelopes to a specific agent at each agency on your list. That gives you more latitude for submitting to other agents at the same agency if a particular agent turns you down; plus, you have a greater possibility of getting more direct attention if you send it to someone specific. Otherwise, it will land on a more general pile at the agency and possibly get overlooked.

HOW TO TRACK YOUR SUBMISSIONS

The best way to track your submissions is to keep three-by-five cards on each of the agencies you submit to. List the agency name, address, and phone number, the specific agent you submitted to, the date, and so on. You will notice in your agent books that they usually say "no calls." They mean it. They don't want people calling. There are so many actors who are looking for agents at the beginning of their careers that the agents just don't have time to give each one the personal attention he would like to have. You can find that out for yourself, though, if you like. Call a few and ask, "Who should I submit to?" They'll tell you to just send it to the agency—not to anyone specific—and if they like it, they'll call you. Submit it to a specific agent anyway. Then, after you've sent in your first thirty or so, wait a week and then call two or three of the agents you submitted to and say, "I'm calling to see if there was any response to the picture and résumé I sent in." And their assistants will say, in essence, *"Dont call us; we'll call you."* But at least you will have satisfied yourself that you have been efficient and that it is, indeed, fruitless to call. Just be sure you have sent a good head shot, a good résumé, and a good cover letter—along with a prayer of great expectation. Then, wait for the agents to call you.

REFERRALS AND RECOMMENDATIONS

Another way to get in the door with an agent, the best way, is to have a recommendation from someone else who is already working in the business. If you know another actor who is represented by the agency you are submitting to and you can get him to call up and recommend you, that can prove helpful as well. Not always, though. The agent may say, "Tell her to send in a picture," and you may just end up in the general stack. But it's always worth a try. If you know someone who is a producer or director and will recommend you, all the better; these people are in the position of later hiring you. Or if you know a casting director who will recommend you, that, too, is terrific because he or she is in the position of later calling you in for auditions.

This means you've got to ask your acquaintance, "Will you please call for me, or write a note or letter of recommendation for me?" You're *asking* for something here, I know. And that may put you in an uncomfortable position because it may make you feel like the other person might think you're a drag. But remember, if you don't self-assert, it won't get done! And if you'd honestly be willing to do this for someone else, you have the spiritual support to ask for this help. Then, once you *are* in the position to do it for someone else, remember those times and how you felt and come through for the people who petition you. So ask for a recommendation. Doing so may prove to be the very way for you to get in the door with a good agent.

THE BRUTAL TRUTH

In the beginning, it appears as if the actor needs the agent more than the agent needs the new actor. This seems reasonable, of course; the agent is employed, for one thing, while the actor is not. But it is not good long-term thinking on the part of the agent to consider the new actor unimportant, and actors never forget it. Nevertheless, it is pretty rare when an agent is truly helpful to an actor when the actor most needs her—at the beginning of his career. Then again, most actors are just giving acting a quick try but aren't really committed to it for the long haul. And most do fall by the wayside. So agents, inundated by these types, have to be choosy. They may blow it from time to time, but they can afford to.

The way it usually works when an agent is mailed an actor's head shot and résumé goes like this: The pictures and résumés— submitted by actors like you who are waiting on pins and needles by the phone—build up into unwieldy stacks until the agent, prompted by her assistant who no longer has any place to put his coffee cup, will say, "Oh, God, I've got to get through these darn pictures!"

"No. No. No. No. No. Maybe. No. Maybe. Yes," says the agent as she quickly sails them to her assistant who then puts them into the three piles of "no," "maybe," and "yes"—the agent having paused only a second to turn the last one over to glance at the résumé before having given it the nod. She continues. "No. No. No. No. Maybe." The maybe's get the once over again, becoming no's or yes's, and that's it. This may be done by a single agent or by committee, but it's done quickly, and when it's over, the assistant staggers with the pile of no's to the trash can, then takes the two or three yes's to his desk and calls and invites those actors to come in for an interview with the agent.

THE INTERVIEW

For four or five months you've sent out your head shots. Finally, you get a phone call from Leo at Commercials Unlimited. He says the agent would like you to come in for an interview. Thrilled, you say "Tanfastic!" and set a time.

When the day comes, go in for your interview with the understanding that the agent *wants* to like you. The agent or agents have already seen something in your photograph and/or résumé that attracted them, and they also must have a space for someone of your type in their stable of actors or they wouldn't have called you. Believe me, they will be tickled pink if you end up filling the bill. So you already have the forces of the universe working for you.

Second, go in as yourself. Do not put on more makeup than you usually wear or dress differently than you usually dress. Go in as yourself and as you have represented yourself in your picture. If you see a discrepancy between the two, blend them. You want to go in looking as close as possible to the way you look in your picture because that's what drew them to you. Above all, be natural. That's who you are and, in the long run, that's all you'll be able to sustain. So, once you have dressed as yourself, go in and be yourself.

Now this is where your Orange Sheet work on your current castability will come in handy. In fact, you might wish to review chapter 12. This is where you deliver your twenty-second sales pitch that says who, as an actor, you are—the way you identify yourself as a marketable product.

✳ EXERCISE

Using your Orange Sheet exercise information (see chapter 12), write another twenty-second monologue that encapsulates who you, as an actor or actress, are.

_____
_____
_____
_____.

Now compare this market monologue with the one you wrote in chapter 12. Are they the same? If not, how has this one evolved?

You're going in as yourself, you're being yourself, and you've got your marketing pitch down. Good. Now what else do you take with you to the interview? Confidence and trust—confidence in yourself and trust that the universal system will ensure the success of the meeting for both of you. Get a good night's sleep the night before, and keep yourself happy and peaceful before you go in. Then go in being your best.

A word about attitude here. Do not go in with the "please take me!" attitude. Some of the smaller agents have chips on their shoulders. They know they will probably be able to keep an actor for only the beginning period of her career because as soon as she gets successful, she will be seduced and probably swept away by a bigger, more powerful agency. Now the small agents have the power; they know that right now _you_ need _them_. But don't buy into that mindset. It is true that you do need an agent. But you need an agent who will work with you with mutual respect and appreciation. You need a reciprocal relationship. You have something to give; they have something to give. So, instead of projecting "please take me," go in as an equal to see if the relationship between you and the agency will be a good one. You are going to show them that you know what your product is and that you are clear about your niche in the play. There are also a few questions that you will want them to answer:

1. You will be telling them about your castability profile, as you see it. You will want to know how they see you. Will they represent you in a way that is consistent with your view of yourself?
2. How many clients do they represent?
3. How many clients like you do they have in their stable?
4. What is the predominant type of work of their clients— film, television, theater, commercials?
5. If you agree to work together, will you be able to come in and look at the breakdowns and recommend yourself for submissions?
6. Will you be able to recommend yourself for submission if you hear about a role from another source?
7. How often can you expect to go out on auditions? What's average for clients of your type?
8. How often may you call them to check in? What's reasonable before they consider you a nudge? (Do they understand that you have to look after your career and can't forever sit idly by a silent phone?)
9. What can you do to help them do their job for you as your representative?
10. Can you take them to lunch once in a while?

Not only is gathering this information necessary for you to decide whether or not this agent is right for you, but doing so will give you an opportunity for you to get to know your prospective agent a bit. Ask your agent something about him- or herself. Again, you are both finding out information and establishing the basis for a relationship.

If they like you and want to go the next step with you, the agent(s) may ask you to prove to them that you can act, in one of three ways: (1) they may ask you to cold read a scene for them; (2) they may ask you to bring in an audition videotape that shows you doing a scene and/or a couple of monologues;

or (3) they may ask you to come back and perform a monologue or scene for them in their office.

Although you might be asked to do a cold reading on the spot, you will almost never be asked to do a monologue or scene without warning. If, by exception, you are; you are perfectly within your rights to say, "I'm not quite prepared. I'd like to come back and do it." That said, however, go in prepared! Go in prepared to do a monologue, be brushed up on your a cold-reading skills, and come in having done your physical and vocal warm-up. If they ask you for a videotape and you don't have one, you have one of two choices. You can say you don't have one, which is a giveaway that you are a beginner—which is fine, but be aware of it—or you can say you'll bring it by later, and then zoom home and get to work on making one. But do as much as you can that first meeting; you might never get in for a second one.

Once the interview is over, the agent will respond in one of three ways. He may say he doesn't think you are right for the agency, which usually doesn't happen because who likes to say that kind of thing face to face? He may say he'll call you and let you know, which usually *means* he doesn't think you are right for the agency, but he doesn't want to say that now. Or he may say "Yes, let's try it," at which point you can start planning your "Hooray!" party.

If he does say let's try it, the agency may offer you a one-year contract, but they probably will not. They'll probably suggest that you just try working together for a couple of months to see what happens. Don't let that discourage you. There is a SAG ruling that if a SAG-affiliated agency doesn't get you an audition within any ninety-day period, that ninety-first day you can walk, whether you have a contract or not. So most agents don't bother with contracts until you get your first job through them. Besides, they know how difficult it is to get an agent in the beginning, so they're not really afraid that you're going to walk.

YOUR AUDITION VIDEOTAPE

If you make an audition videotape, keep it short—no more than ten minutes—and simple. Have your name at the head, follow it with one or two short monologues and one or two scenes (each piece preceded by its title) and have your name at the end. That's it. Three or four pieces are plenty; ten minutes, maximum. The same way that agents zoom through their stacks of head shots, they zoom through their stacks of videos, which take even more of their precious time. They watch an actor do one thing for a few seconds, fast forward and watch him do something else, then they eject the tape and move on to the next one. So, short and sweet. Give them just enough to let them know that you know what you are doing. You usually won't get these tapes back, either, so make sure that you keep the master. Don't distribute them indiscriminately because, unless specifically requested, they won't even be looked at, let alone returned to you.

❀ *Affirmation*

> *I am now being led to the right agent(s) who will be delighted to represent me. Thank you, God.*

PERSONAL MANAGERS

If the agent is the sales manager in your career, the manager is your marketing expert. "Why should I give an agent 10 percent and then a manager 15 percent of what I make?" you may ask. "That's 25 percent of my gross income!"

Isn't keeping 75 percent of a real pie better than keeping 100 percent of nothing? It is. Besides, those are success problems; we like those. "I've got to give 10 percent to my agent and 15 to my manager and 5 to my attorney and 2 to my publicist. Not to mention what I'm going to have to give to the feds!" If you have the volume of business that requires that much of a support team, what exactly do you have to complain about? Besides, once you're at that level, you'll probably also have a good business manager—whom you'll also have to pay!—to help you keep your tremendous expenses in line.

This is just the cost of doing business. Jack Nicholson once told me that he had no problem with paying his taxes. When he received one of his seven- or eight-figure checks he simply figured out how much of that he owed to the government and wrote out a check to them then and there—handling both transactions, the deposit and the tax payment, on the same day. Then he never had to spend any time feeling anxious over it. He was done with it. So don't choose not to have a manager simply because you think he may cost too much. A good manager can more than compensate for what he costs you. But do you have to have a manager to succeed as an actor? No.

Some people think that a performer only needs a manager if he has a multifaceted career. If you are a comedian, as well as an actor, singer, and writer, and you have different agents and different sources of income for each of those categories, then it might be very helpful for you to have a manager to oversee and coordinate all the activities and financial matters arising from each source. And yet, many actors who are strictly actors have managers in addition to having agents. Some have *only* managers. Why? What can a manager do for you that an agent cannot?

A manager, usually, represents fewer clients than an agent does. That is because a manager spends more time and effort in developing the careers of his clients than an agent does. A manager is not supposed to solicit work for his clients but most often do. Or if he doesn't personally submit you, he will call your agent and ask her to do so—if you have an agent. If you do not, a good manager will help you secure one. Your manager's belief in you—plus the fact that he is willing to spend his time and effort in helping you on speculation—serves as a strong endorsement and recommendation to an agent. This is a tremendous advantage to you as a newcomer. In addition, a good manager will consider the various facets and assets of your career and find ways in which to help you develop and further your work; whereas an agent's activities are usually restricted to submitting you for auditions and negotiating offers when you get the parts. Whether or not you should have a manager, however, is a question only you can answer. If you answer yes, here's how to go about getting one:

GETTING A MANAGER

As with agents, lists of managers are out there, although not as many. Henderson in New York puts out a good one. It's available through Samuel French, Drama Bookshop, and Applause, among other stores. You submit your pictures and résumés to them just like you do to agents. In this case, however, I suggest that you call them first. They might ask you to simply submit your head shot, but if so, in that case I recommend that you enclose a more detailed letter explaining how you see your career developing and why you are seeking a manager. Like with agents, if you have a referral, you have a greater likelihood of getting in for an interview.

If they do ask you to come in for an interview, go in like you do with agents as a businessperson, knowing who you are and what you can do. And remember, you will always be your own best self-asserting salesperson, even after you have secured the best team of representatives available; you must love your product, yourself, or you will never be able to sell it to anyone.

MANAGEMENT CONTRACTS

Be careful in executing contracts with personal managers. If you haven't auditioned in ninety days, you can get out of the contract with your agent, but the contract with your manager has no such loophole. Most managers will ask you to sign either a two- or three-year contract with them. I would ask you to beware of signing a contract for longer than a year. Sometimes two is OK, but don't go for three. Three years is a long time. A lot can happen in your career in three years. Two should be sufficient, and one is preferable. Your manager, of course, will want it to be longer so that she can reap some of the rewards of her early nurturing efforts, and that makes sense. But you don't want to be stuck in low gear for three years if you are not making any headway. If your manager can't do anything to help you within one or two years, then bail. And if she can and does, then re-sign for another year or two. I believe a good, confident manager will feel comfortable with that. She'll feel that she will be so good for you that you'll be begging her to continue to represent you. I like that kind of confidence. It's good American business. You and your manager should continue in business together only if the relationship is proving to be beneficial for you both.

A WORD OF CAUTION

Sometimes managers will ask you to pay them to represent you. I don't like that. I don't see anything immoral about it, but if you make that kind of arrangement you're making a different kind of deal—one that, in my opinion, is far from ideal.

The standard manager/client arrangement works this way: the manager represents you on speculation until you start making money, from which he—like your agent—then takes his cut. He—like your agent does—pays all his own expenses. He doesn't charge you for any of it. He invests his time and effort in you because he believes in your earning potential that he is agreeing to develop and then manage. He gets nothing at first but, because of his faith in you, he later gets his whopping 15 percent.

Managers who charge you a fee, however, don't have the same level of investment in you. You are a sure source of income to them from the beginning. They don't have to farm their belief in you—which is what you *want* your manager to do— to get paid. They don't have to do much at all; they're already getting paid. What you are paying them is a fee to cover a portion of their overhead and operating expenses, and their *intention* to *try* to help you—rather than commission on the work they helped you to get. The manager's incentive in an arrangement of this kind is weak from the point of view of the actor. Sometimes this type of arrangement is suggested by a manager who is new in the business; he can't yet afford to work without charging his clients a fee. You may think that this person is trustworthy and decide to work along with him this way for a while. That's up to you. Just be sure that you are clear about what he is offering you in exchange for the monthly fee he is charging you, and that you feel you will be getting your money's worth.

REPRESENTING YOURSELF

Since it takes time to get an agent and/or a manager, what can you do for yourself in the meantime? Can you do anything?

Because of the way the business is structured, you can't go very far without an agent, but yes, you can get somewhere. Here are a few suggestions:

1. Attend open casting calls that you hear about over the breakdowns or via the trades, such as *The Hollywood Reporter, Variety,* or *Back Stage.*

2. Promote yourself directly to filmmakers by offering to work as an actor, which is preferable, of course, or as a crew member.
3. Visit casting directors who hold generals—open calls (once a week or once a month) in which actors are invited to drop by and introduce themselves. If you sense some rapport with any of them, ask them if they might recommend an agent for you to contact. This is difficult to pull off because they are inundated with such requests; but if you can, it's great because a recommendation from a casting director carries a lot of weight. At least get known by these casting directors. Then you can tell agents that you know this or that casting director, which will help you secure an agent.
4. Do plays.
5. Put together a one-man or one-woman show.
6. Submit yourself for student films. The casting notices are published in *Back Stage* and other trades. The filmmakers usually pay their actors by giving them a copy of the film, which can then be added to the actor's audition reel.
7. Send out cards announcing your performances to casting directors, agents, managers, producers, and directors, letting them know that you are doing this work. Get your name out there. Again, in advertising, the experts tell us a product has to be introduced or presented to the potential consumer three times before it sticks in the consumer's mind, at which point not only does it stick, but the consumer feels he has a personal relationship with the product. In promoting yourself, therefore, utilize this marketing strategy: Be visible.
8. Pay to be part of a showcase. This can be expensive, but it is an option. I know of one well-produced showcase, for example, that, for 400 dollars, allows you the opportunity to come in with your scene and scene partner

and be part of a four-night run for the purpose of attracting agents and managers who come looking for new clients. A friend of mine just picked up a good commercial agent through his participation there. It cost him the 400 dollars, but he is now represented by one of the best commercial agencies in Los Angeles.

There is much that you can do before you secure an agent or a manager. And there is much that you must continue to do once you have representation. Don't ever sit back, thinking that you have successfully abdicated your responsibility to your support staff. It is *your* career. As John Cusak said, you must be a leader. You must lead your team of representatives and other support staff in the collective effort of promoting and managing your career. Otherwise, you will get—in a word—screwed. Someone will drop the ball, which will be exactly what you will have deserved because you never should have let it out of your hands.

HOW TO SEE YOUR REPRESENTATIVES

Your representatives are your employees, whether you pay them or not. They will never be paying you. You may not get work for a while, and therefore during that time, they will be working on spec for you; nevertheless, when you do get work *you* pay *them*. They will collect your money for you and take their percentage of it before passing the balance on to you; but it is from *your* money that they are paid. They work for you. And the sooner you develop this attitude with grace, and respect—and unmistakable clarity—the sooner it will pay off in success for all of you. Don't ever let them think they are doing you a favor. They're not. Believe me, not one of those people is going to take you on to do you a favor. They will take you on because they think you can make them money, which is how it should be.

See your representatives, then, as your helpers who see your value. They're purpose in your life is to help you promote your career. They are not artists; you cannot expect them to have the artistic vision that you do or to fully understand your vision. It is your place to have that vision and transmit it to them as clearly as possible. But then it is their job to go into the marketplace and sell it.

Once your reps have signed on, support them in any way that you can to help them promote you. Don't make it hard for them. If they get you an interview, don't be a schmo and say that you don't do interviews. Actors work against themselves and everyone who has signed on to help them when they pull this kind of immature, egocentric baloney. Be clear about what you will and won't do at the time you make your agreements, and then keep yours. Otherwise, people are going to think you're a jerk, which is not going to help your career.

Love your representatives. I can't overemphasize the importance of this. Express your love tangibly by occasionally sending them gifts, notes of appreciation, flowers, the perfect knickknack, chocolate cake, or tickets to something delightful. Use your imagination, which shouldn't be hard for you. You are an expert at that. You are an artist, an actor!

WHEN DO YOU START LOOKING FOR AN AGENT?

Now. Look for your agents now. Go out on auditions now. Begin the process now. It may take a while, so there's no good reason to wait. When you realize that it may take a while, you will be better able to relax into the ongoing process. Be diligent and trusting, and you will succeed. You are supply; therefore you are in demand. You are perfectly representative of a large contingent of humanity; therefore you will be well represented. You understand the human condition; therefore, you will be well appreciated. It is your inspired work to be an actor. Therefore, individuals whose work it is to represent actors will be inspired, by the same consciousness that inspires you, to see your value and *want* to represent you. And you can begin that whole process right now!

❋ EXERCISE

Be sixteen years old again and answer the question, What do you want to be when you grow up?

____

____

SUMMARY OF MAIN POINTS

1. You do need representation to get out on the calls that bring in the money. Agents, managers, and your own personal resources are the three sources of representation from which you can draw.
2. It is most productive to look for a small- or mid-sized agency at first, for an agent who needs you as much as you need him or her.
3. A good head shot, résumé, and cover letter are the three elements that constitute your mail-in submissions to agents and managers.
4. In addition to having a great head shot and an impressive résumé, a great way to get in the door with an agent is to have a recommendation from someone who is already working in the business.
5. You will have to assert yourself to ask for a recommendation. But remember, an actor must self-assert to succeed. If you are willing to help someone who asks for your help, you have the spiritual support to ask others to help you.

6. Go in to the interview with your prospective representative with the understanding that he or she wants to like you. Show up *as* yourself, *be* yourself, and *love* yourself as well as the people on the other side of the desk.

7. Prepare well for your interviews. Know your actor's sales pitch, be prepared to do a monologue, be sharp on your cold-reading skills and go in having done your physical and vocal warm-up.

8. You will always be your own best salesperson, before and after you secure your representatives. Get comfortable with that. Never sit back and abdicate the responsibility for your career to anyone else.

9. Start looking for an agent right now!

CHAPTER 21

The Successful Audition

It is not because things are difficult that we do not dare; it is because we do not dare that they are difficult.

—Seneca

AUDITIONS ARE NOT REHEARSALS

The actor really begins to work when he or she auditions. An audition is not a tryout, a rehearsal, or even a practice; it is the real thing—an acting job—and you get one shot at it. So, how do you go about doing it well?

The first thing to do before any audition, of course, is to prepare yourself mentally. I say "of course" because by now I'm sure I've made clear my belief that, to remain *on* course, daily mental preparation must become standard procedure. The quickest route to success, then, is by making your first business meeting of every day a meeting with your source. After you have reaffirmed for yourself your worth as a person and as an actor, that good is operating, and that, regardless of the outcome, your audition will be successful, then you are ready to attend to some of the mechanics of the process of auditioning.

✳ EXERCISE

Please list three components of a successful audition:

1. _____
2. _____
3. _____

✳ EXERCISE

Please write five affirmations about your auditions that you would like to be true:

1. _____
2. _____
3. _____
4. _____
5. _____

Now affirm, with joy, how true they already are.

THE MECHANICS OF THE SUCCESSFUL AUDITION

One of the worst things that you can feel when you get to an audition is to feel rushed! Fortunately, with a little planning, you can avoid that. Get there early. If your audition is set for ten o'clock, get there at nine-fifteen. Sign up, get comfortable in the waiting room, look at the people around you, love them, and realize that they are not your enemies but are on the same cosmic road you are on, working toward the same goals of understanding and dominion. Not one of them has the power to prevent you from receiving all that life intends for you.

Then take a look at the sides (the pages you will be reading in the audition). You will be dealing with just a fraction of the script, so you will be given only a small, and perhaps misleading, amount of information as to what's going on in it, but to the best of your ability, you will have to determine the following: Who is this person, your character? What does he or she want? What are the conflicts and obstacles frustrating his or her desires? And what is he or she willing to do to overcome those obstacles? That's a lot to do in a short amount of time; you will be making some snap judgments, but you can do it.

Then slowly, methodically read the scene one word at a time. Don't succumb to the temptation to memorize the thing. Just explore. Get familiar with the text, slowly. Once you feel familiar with it, begin to read your character's words out loud. Find a corner, outside if necessary, and read it aloud so you can hear the sound of your own voice speaking your character's words before you go in and read for the director.

If you have a difficult time with reading, make sure you arrive extra early to practice. If you have a heavy accent, or difficulty with the accent assigned to the character, give yourself enough time to practice. Many of my students are from other countries and some of them have difficulty with American accents and pronunciations. Be aware of these challenges if you have them. Arrive early and ask someone who speaks English well if you're saying a word correctly and if your emphasis is correct. Make sure you know what every word means and, of course, have a specific meaning for everything that you say. Then, as I recommended in chapter 15, practice reading the scene with another actor who is there to audition and is willing to practice with you. Not all actors will be willing to do this, but you'll be doing a service for the one who accepts your invitation; you'll be preparing him as well as yourself. And not only will you both become practiced in your parts, you'll also get the butterflies out of your stomach (or at least into formation) and your breath regulated before you go in.

BEING TRUE TO YOUR INSTINCTS

When you read for a part, perform it as if your director has said, "You already have the part and can do it any way you want to." That's what you go in with. That's your strength.

If, on the other hand, you go in thinking that you're going to try to give them what you think *they* want, you will be completely off your base. First of all, you don't know what they want; second, you'll be forfeiting your confidence in your choices—you won't be *making* any choices; and third, you'll be flagging your insecurity. That will not get you the part. But if you go in confident in *your* take on the part, then they will either like that and hire you, or not. Naturally, you should be receptive to trying any adjustments that the director requests, but, in the main, do it your way. Working that way will ensure that there will be enough times when people will hire you to constitute a satisfying career for you. Perhaps even the same people who may not hire you for this gig—but will have witnessed how professional and self-possessed you were when auditioning—will call you for something else in the future. One thing is certain: The parts you do get will be because the people really did want *you*. Those parts will be in concert with who you really are, as a person and as an actor—and that you will find most satisfying.

YOU ARE BESTOWING THE FAVOR

Remember, too, that you are doing producers and directors a favor when you go in and audition for a part, and not the other way around. You are reading this part for them, giving them your interpretation of how it should be done, *for free*. So don't let anyone intimidate you with any disrespectful power games. The good ones won't try to, but others will. Don't let them. Just love the little creeps until they cool it. Walk in, not with the attitude that they owe you anything, because they don't—you've agreed to do it for free—but do not feel they have any power over you. You have one thing to concentrate on—and that is to be clear about what you mean and then mean it when you deliver your lines. Do love every one in the room, but then get on with it. Stand or sit where the director tells you to stand or sit, make friendly eye contact with your scene partner, and then live your part.

Don't crave the part, though. You're fine if you get it, and you're fine if you don't. You are simply offering your services here because doing so is part of your work. If they can use you, fine. If not, that's OK, too. And when they say thank you, don't grovel and say, "Oh, thank *you!*" Graciously say, "You're welcome."

Having worked this way, you can then leave the audition with that wonderful comforting Zen mindset of having done the work and now forgetting it. Because you were, you *are*, successful. You gave a wonderful audition performance, you kept your power, you loved, and you trusted. Now it is over. And let it be over. Don't check your answering service or machine every five minutes to see if you got the part. If they want you, they'll call you, and they'll give you plenty of time to get back to them.

✳ EXERCISE

Agree to audition for something once a week for the next four weeks. Please signify your agreement to do this by signing below.

Agreed: _____

DEEPENING YOUR COMMITMENT TO ACTING

Let's talk more about the actor's commitment—your commitment—to acting as an art, a business, and a calling.

Just about the time you start thinking you've been working too hard, that you've been spending too much time thinking, praying, studying, training, rehearsing, calling, mailing, and auditioning, that's when it's time to *deepen* your commitment to making your acting your livelihood. Every time it seems difficult, like you've gotten more rejection than all the other actors in the world combined and have already exceeded your limits of self-exertion and patience and trust, it's time, not to run away or throw in the towel, but to deepen your commitment. It's time to turn those moments of despair into moments of rebirth. And you can do so because it is when you are the most down that you are the most ready to spring up again. If you want to succeed, you must.

This concept of commitment is a powerful one and it works across the boards of your acting as your art, your business, and your calling.

COMMITMENT TO ACTING AS AN ART

When you are on stage and lose your concentration, if you commit more fully to your action—fueled by your governing intention and feelings—not only will you bring yourself back on track, but you will nail yourself to the heart of the moment with such fixity that there will be no further danger of wavering during the rest of that performance.

Commitment, connection, meaning. Commitment connects you to your meaning, the definite, unhesitant going-for-it. Commit, therefore, to acting as an art. Commit first to learning what the art of acting is. The moment you think you've got it down, be a child and discover more. Keep the awe, the wonder, the *art* of acting alive in your heart. Read the master teachers and practitioners of the art of acting. Spend an evening reading what Michael Caine has to say about the differences between film and stage acting, or read Laurence Olivier's memoirs, or what Katharine Hepburn says about how to succeed in the world of drama. It will be like having them over for dinner except that you won't have to cook and they won't waste your time with small talk. And listen to what newcomers to acting say they think acting is, why they are attracted to it, and what they love about it. Via their innocence and naïveté, fresh insights will be revealed to you: You will realize that you know more about acting than you thought you did, as well as how much it is a part of your life.

Reaffirm for yourself that acting is your chosen form of self-expression. Sometimes when we get caught up in the business of acting, or even in the mission of acting, we forget the joyful aspect of acting as a means of expressing ourselves for self-fulfillment and fun. Acting gives us a sense of innocent and delightful play in the kingdom. We get to pretend, make believe, be anyone and everyone. So go ahead, recommit. Dip your creative toe into every pool of life. Live hundreds of lives in your one. That is what acting is as an art, the ability to expand your sense of yourself into every self, all selves, the one overall collective self. Acting as an art is the thrill of making your own decisions about how a particular state of mind should be represented, and then making yourself believe that you really are all that the assignment calls for. You are a queen. You are a slave. You are a priest or priestess. You are a wealthy heiress, a dispossessed heir, a skillful thief. You are a mass murderer. You are an avatar. You are every archetype within the human consciousness, and you give yourself permission to make believe that you are all of them. Acting is a natural expansion of our sense of ourselves. It is your art and you do it well, with love, compassion, and awareness. Deepen your commitment to your art.

COMMITMENT TO ACTING AS A BUSINESS

Deepen, also, your commitment to acting as a business. Mean it in the business arena as intensely as you mean business on stage. We have to make a living by contributing something of value, that we love doing, to the system, and the system compensates us with our living. Acting is your business; it is the way you contribute to the community, for which the community pays you.

Say to yourself, "I am a businessperson. Acting is my business. I do it for many reasons, one of which is to make money. I expect my activities in this business to succeed in making me a good living. There's need for the supply that I, as an artist, am, because society must have dramatic acting to understand truth and to prosper."

Every business has standards and practices by which it operates that facilitate the daily workings of the business. In acting, these include the ways one goes about learning one's craft, getting an agent, and so on. These practices do *not* include operating with hesitancy or lack of commitment. Yet many people going into acting say, "I'll give it a year or two and see what happens." What are you doing when you do that? Not only are you allowing for the possibility that you may fail, you are *planning* for it, sabotaging your success at the outset. But you don't have to; you have been given dominion within the Earth experience, and the world will obey you.

Attend to your business daily. Figure out how it works. Do what it takes. Make yourself proficient in your business of acting. Refine and improve your product if you think it needs it— pick up some training in improvisation or cold reading, become more comfortable with comedy, cut your hair, work out, drop some weight—whatever it takes. Deepen your commitment to the business of acting and attend to that business daily.

COMMITMENT TO ACTING AS A CALLING

Remember that acting is a calling. Remind yourself that it is an important work that you are undertaking every time you pick up a piece of text and begin to explore its meaning. Deepen that commitment. Realize that the work is grand and commit to staying with it as your mission.

That really is the whole point of deepening your commitment to your art, your business, and your calling: the daily reinforcing of your dedication to staying with it. You have chosen acting as your way of self-expression, your way of contributing to the world and making a living, and your way of serving God. Sometimes this choice comes easily. Most of the time, though, it is a decision, or revelation, that will have taken blood, sweat, and *years* to manifest. Don't abandon it because it's not easy. Renew your dedication. Say you will work hard throughout your life and get better at the art of acting. Say you will stay with it as your business, as your way to interact with and contribute to society. Say you will stay with it as your calling. It is your calling, the way that you serve truth. And by deepening your commitment and fidelity to acting as an art, a business, and a calling, you will strengthen the inevitability of your getting better and better at it. You will be on your way to eventually having achieved that great satisfaction of knowing that while you were on Earth, you got really good at something that you loved doing and that really mattered.

✳ EXERCISE

Write a short paragraph in which you express your renewed commitment to your acting as an art, a business, and a calling. Then sign it. Read the paragraph to someone you trust and ask him or her to sign it as a witness.

SUMMARY OF MAIN POINTS

1. You must prepare for your auditions spiritually and technically for them to be successful and satisfying.
2. Trust your artistic instincts and keep your own power strong. Audition as if you already have the part plus carte blanche on your delivery of it. Then adjust if you are willing to, but remember that you are the artist. Maintain your artistic integrity.
3. Remember, too, that you are doing the casting director, director, and producers who are auditioning you a favor. You are giving them your expert interpretation of the role, for free. So do not let anyone intimidate you with any disrespectful power games.
4. Deepen your commitment to acting as an art, a business, and a calling. Commitment fastens you to your intention and meaning; it is the unhesitant going-for-it. You are doing a grand work; stay with it and you will succeed.

Part IV

WHY YOU
DO IT

*Acknowledging Acting
As Your Calling*

CHAPTER 22

Acting As Your Mission or Calling

An actor is either a high priest or a clown.
—Oscar Wilde

A cting is a calling that is as worthy of reverence and respect as is the calling of being a doctor, a minister, a nun, a therapist, or an artist in any other medium. In the most profound sense, the mission of each one of us is simply to be who we really are, to express the divine nature in our own unique and distinct way. Acting as a profession provides a wonderful means for its practitioners to do this—for actors simply act like people act.

✷ EXERCISE

If you are over twenty-one, be twenty-one years old again and answer the following questions. What do you want to do with the rest of your life?

_____

_____

Are you on your target?_____

If you are not on your target, why not?

_____

_____

THE UNIVERSE GOVERNS BY DESIRE

You know your calling by checking in with yourself and truthfully answering the question, what would I like to do? Not what do you think you *should* do, but what would you *like* to do. What do you think would be the most fun? The most exciting to you? The most delightful to you? What would feel, not necessarily the easiest, but the most natural to you? If you answer that you would like to be an actor on stage or in front of the camera, then that is the will of God for you, the will of your highest sense of yourself speaking to you.

Although the types of occupations we can engage in are limited by the extent of the human experience, every occupation provides the insights prescribed for us to get here on Earth and furthers us along our spiritual journey. This proves that the greatest reward we can reap from any occupation is the growth that the occupation demands of us. To that extent, any of the occupations will do, *if you like doing it.*

✵ EXERCISE

Climb into a hot bath, the hotter the better. Then allow yourself to become sad, compassionate, grief-stricken. Bring up from your psyche memories or images that make you sad. Feed these memories, deepen them, until they make you cry.

At first, you may have to fake the crying. Make crying sounds and at the same time feed the effort by thinking more deeply about whatever will contribute to making you cry.

Think about the sorrow in your past, the things you wish you had or hadn't done; think about the cruelty of man to man, of man to animals. Cry and feed the feeling until you are sobbing. Remember, this is an acting exercise. This will show you that you have control over your emotions and prove to you that you can bust the emotional blockage (especially if you are a man) that says, "Don't cry!" and that, when you need to, you will be able to cry on command.

Then, when you have had a good and thorough cry, finish by knowing that this exercise is beneficial to you as an actor and that it will have no ill effects on you. Believe me— that will hardly be a concern; you will feel fabulous! This exercise not only allows you to prove to yourself your dominion over your emotions, but it is tremendously empathetic and cathartic.

JOBS ALONG THE WAY

We may have to take additional temporary jobs to put food on the table before we succeed in making our full living from acting. For instance, if while you are working toward being an actor, Uncle John offers you a job in his hardware store, it might be a good idea for you to take it. You need the money; working in a hardware store won't drain you of your creative juices like many other jobs; and he will probably let you off for auditions. On the other hand, it might be helpful for you to choose a day job that is more directly connected to acting. With a little imagination and willingness, you will think of, or recognize, the perfect temporary day job for you.

RECOGNIZING YOUR HEART'S DESIRE

"Fine," you might say, "I can recognize the right *day* job. But how do I choose my *career* if I want to be several things and can't decide?"

This is not an uncommon problem The rule of thumb I find most effective is to choose the career that makes you blush when you admit it to others, the one that, to you, seems the most grand. If the little demons—using your own voice—say, "That's only my ego talking when I say I want to be that!" that's a good indication that that is exactly the career for you.

VINDICATING YOUR MOTIVES

But, you may be thinking, I want to be an actor for primarily selfish reasons. Well, I don't buy that. I believe that your deepest reasons are unselfish and that this nasty self-accusation is just another demonic decoy to your happiness. OK, it may *appear* to you that your primary motivation to act consists of the threefold desire for power, fame, and money—and I congratulate you on your honesty if you admit that it does. But if you are *really* honest, I believe you will admit that your main goal is to do something good. Why is it so hard to admit *that* fact to ourselves or another? I'll tell you why. If you think you are being self-centered by wanting material success, the ego *really* goes nuts when it hears that you want to act to help people; it says now you're being grandiose—not to mention full of baloney.

Give yourself a break. Your deepest desire is to give, to help, to make a difference. Because that's who you are. You are love—conscious, living love. OK, so you also want the perks. What's wrong with that? Life is your employer. The perks are life's way of keeping its employees happy so that life continues to function perfectly.

THE EFFICIENCY OF AUTHENTIC DESIRE

Governing by desire is a most efficient way to run the universe. With each individual designed and motivated to self-govern, it's brilliant! Each manifestation of being, from the smallest to the biggest, has its own universally supported desires and aspirations as well as its own inner guidance toward their inevitable fulfillment. Desire is a potent force, a *good* force. Just be very clear about what it is that you do want.

Sometimes we think we want something we don't, or don't anymore. We go traipsing off after the first desire that occurs to us only to find that getting it muddles our peace of mind. You see a young child on the street happily licking an ice cream cone and suddenly you want one too. But on closer examination, you may discover that you don't really want ice cream. What you are really seeking is a childlike playfulness and what would satisfy you better than an ice cream cone would be to go out and buy yourself a pad of paper and a box of crayons. The desire for ice cream was a knee-jerk reaction. The ice cream represented fun to you, but you wanted fun in a different form.

So, think about what it is that you do want. Then, once you've determined that your desire is sincere, go for it. True desire will not lead you wrong; it keeps things moving forward, and it keeps you grounded on your path. Desire will lead you home.

❈ EXERCISE

Find a short fairy tale written for young children—a tale that you like—and then read it to a three- to five-year-old child (your own child, a niece, nephew, a neighbor). As you read, notice the dynamics that you employ: full commitment to the dramatics to hold their interest, full enunciation to communicate clearly, full emotional expression to compensate for your young reader's limited vocabulary, and enthusiasm. And note your lack of self-consciousness, because you know that your audience is not judging you. Then determine to use what you have learned from this exercise in your future performances for adult audiences.

DESIRE HAS A TEMPORARY OFF SWITCH

In the arts—particularly acting and singing—it is a common thing to be "on it" for a while and then "off" for a while. You act, going after it in a fury for a time, then you don't want to do it for a while. You sing every day for weeks, then you don't sing for two months. But this is natural. You need a break here and there so that you can renew your energies in the same way that an artichoke field needs to be planted with mustard between crops to replenish it with certain necessary minerals. For the artist, it is during the off period that desire to produce again begins to emerge, enhanced with fresh insight gathered and assimilated while resting. This puts you back on the path of production—which you were never really off because the path requires this periodic resting.

So when you don't want to work on your acting, don't. Rest. When you begin to want to work on it again, do. Trust your desires. They won't lead you wrong. The only thing wrong regarding desire is one's failure to listen to and be guided by it.

BUT HOW DO I KNOW IT'S FOR ME?

How do I really know, though, if acting is for me? How do I know that it is not just a passing fantasy, a temporary infatuation?

Even if it does appear but a passing fantasy, indulge it. If you can honestly say you really would like to try it for a short period to see if you like it well enough to continue to do it, that is your permission—your instruction, in fact—to proceed. Once you are doing it, the fantasy may prove to be not so passing after all. Even if it does pass, it will not have been a waste of your time; it will have been a useful bridge to your next activity. In either case, though, if you feel like doing it—for however long you feel like it—go for it. "Feeling like it" is how you know it's for you. If you feel like it's your calling, you're right. If you feel like it may be your calling, you are right again; it may be.

If you feel like it may not be your calling, however, you may not be right; that feeling may be just resistance. Check that one out very carefully. If your answer is a simple no because other things turn you on more, then move on to one of those other things. But if your no is charged with strong negative emotional energy (I definitely don't want to do that! You'll never get *me* up on stage!), it is likely that fear is blocking your desire. The truth is you would like to try it, but you're scared. If that's the case, you owe it to yourself to bolster your courage and try it.

✺ EXERCISE

If you are over thirty, be thirty years old again and answer the following questions.

What do you want to do with the rest of your life?

_____

_____

Are you on your target?_____

If you are not on your target, why not?_____

_____

Now be yourself at your present age and answer the following questions.

What do you want to do with the rest of your life?

_____

_____

Are you on your target?_____

If you are not on your target, why not?_____

_____

GENTLY, BUT FIRMLY, DOES IT

Sometimes our passion carries us along and we think, "Yes, damn it, I don't care what comes up! I'm going to do what I really want to do, no matter what!" We try to employ _will_ as a substitute for true desire, or think we need to force things with all our might to execute our desire. But it can be much easier than that. Don't be afraid to just say, "I want it." Don't be afraid that the universe is then going to say, "Then you can't have it. Somebody else gets it, but not you. _You_ have to do something you don't want to do."

Don't be afraid—or _be_ afraid and do it anyway. Say what you really want. Treat the universe as a huge, beneficent, spiritual smorgasbord. Walk up to it with your empty bowl and say, "Yes, I'll have some of that and some of that, please." Trust that this smorgasbord exists to fulfill your every desire, because that, in fact, is the truth. So don't worry that you won't get what you want. Take the stand that you _will_ get what you want, then humbly ask for it.

Know, too, that if you take something back to your table and discover that it is bitter and that you don't want it after all, you don't have to finish it. You may cancel your order. Grab another bowl, walk back up to the table, and select something else. And you may do this as many times as you want. If you approach your desires with this open, trusting, fearless, _guiltless_ attitude, you will first, easily discern what your desires are; second, have more courage to ask for them; and third, will not be afraid that you will get stuck doing something in life that you don't want to.

ALL PARTS IN THE SYSTEM ARE OF EQUAL VALUE

In the system of spirit, the contributions of us all are equally valuable because they are all constituted of the same substance: consciousness working, not at cross purposes, but in harmony because life is an indivisible unit. *None* of it could exist if *all* of it didn't exist in its entirety. Your contribution may be to clean and polish silverware, or to be a security guard so that you have the time to read every book you've ever wanted to read, or to be a nanny so you may enjoy the company of a small child and his family. However seemingly modest or grand your contributions may be, as long as they come from your true desire you can be sure that they are needed and valued in the system. What is important, then, is that you feel happy with what you choose to do.

SELFISHNESS IS THE LEAST SELFISH OF ALL

"I've always been my own child," said Alec McCowen. "I think an actor needs to be. It also helps to be extremely selfish. You have to have space to work."

You do your best for others when you are doing what you want to do. This is very important. If you select your work based on what you believe other people want you to do, you are committing a mortal sin because it will kill your spirit. The heck with other people when it comes to that! Other people neither know nor have the right to tell you what to do; nor do they really care. Nor is that way of deciding what to do the way of the universe. A kitten does not do what a dog wants him to do, any more than the dog does what the kitten wants him to. Nor are you forced to do—nor should you *obey*—what you think your mother wants you to do, or your father wants you to do, or Jesus wants you to do—even what you think *God* wants you to do! That may sound sacrilegious and untrue, but it isn't. Yes, you want to do God's will, and so do I, but you don't do God's will by considering God an entity outside yourself and then trying to figure out what that entity thinks and wills. On the contrary, you do God's will by trusting that God has put within your consciousness—via your desires—your personal guidance and direction, and you follow *that*. You do God's will by doing your own. That means you get to do what you truly want to do. Isn't that a terrific way to run things?

The so-called sin of selfishness, then, is a misteaching. It is preached by uptight men and women who dress in high collars, wear their hair in tight buns, have sharp pointy noses, and never get laid. It is a lie that says the will is evil and chooses only evil, that it is a sin to go after what you want, that it is better to suffer and sacrifice. Look at what that is saying about our creator. It's saying that our creator has created us with faulty, misshapen wills. Remember, just as there is one mind, there is one will. Therefore, your will and God's will is the same one will. The will is good, and—as you will notice in your own experience and that of your children—it rebels and becomes violent *only* when it is stifled. It becomes violent not because it is *ex*pressed but because it is *re*pressed.

You will run into people who don't want you to do what you want to do because they didn't do what they wanted. Watch out for this. But most of all, focus on your work. Do what you want to do. It takes time to figure that out, let alone to start doing it, so get on the path right now.

✖ EXERCISE

Tell an embarrassing moment to a stranger; improvise, making it sound like a natural part of the conversation. This is a great inhibition buster.

A NOTE ON SAVING THE WORLD

We have a planet that needs saving, some people say, and *you* want to be an *actor?!*

The world is already saved, thank you. You don't save the world. You love the world. You do that by being in the world and shining. Don't let other people's fear that everything is terrible blow you away. Don't get caught up in the idea of saving the world. That is a wet blanket that would keep you from the joys of life. The world is already saved. And Jesus didn't save it, either. The world is working just fine. It's got plenty of challenges, but those challenges exist to help *you* grow stronger. And you're ready to face every one of them, none of which has the power to stop you. Nor is anyone going to blow up the world, either. Our world is a spiritual manifestation of the concept of place that resides in our consciousness, continually emitting itself into existence. Not even the meanest or dumbest of us can destroy it. We are learning, but we're not going to blow life up. Life is foolproof, and God is infinitely tolerant. So relax and contribute. I believe the best way to honor and delight our creator is to blossom and serve our brothers and sisters as role models.

The practical advice that serves us, then, is, relax and enjoy the process. That's what our common parent wants. What do you say to *your* children? You can't be a basketball star. You can't be an artist. No, you may not learn to play the piano. No, you can't be a mountain climber. You can't do anything self-fulfilling or fun, certainly nothing you *want* to do. You have to clean up other people's garbage, because the people before you screwed everything up! That's what you're saying when you tell people, or yourself, to save the world—that God and His first-born already blew it for the rest of us before we ever got here.

Our creator isn't that much of a dope! Nor has she programmed us to buy into that line of fear. Tell people who try to lay that on you, "Then *you* go ahead and save the world. Because *I'm* going to have fun over here." This doesn't mean that you're going to ignore suffering; you're not. Acting is your way of alleviating it. *You* are going to make the world better by being great!

※ *Affirmation*

> *I am on my path, in my right place, doing my right work. All is well and I am at peace.*

SINCE IT'S SAVED, NOW WHAT?

Since the world is saved, it is our privileged function to live according to that wonderful fact. By doing so, we are going to make it evident to others that life does operate perfectly; that life, here and now, is good; that Earth is a joyful, wonderful, safe place to be. Our planet is not sick, nor is it our job to heal it. It is our job to contribute to its ongoing well-being by making our contribution of personal magnificence to it.

Rabinadranath Tragore, a great Indian saint and guru to Paramahansa Yogananda, put it this way: "God respects me when I pray but He loves me when I sing." Sing. Write. Paint. Dance. Act! Honor life by expressing its beauty, truth, and love. That is how you do your job as an artist, and that is how you keep our planet healthy because that is how *you* have a happy life and, at the same time, inspire others to do the same. Life is spectacular. If we have a responsibility in all this—and we do—it is to never allow anyone to deflect us from our wonderful and noble purpose of being fabulous!

239

CLAIMING YOUR RIGHT TO BE AN ACTOR

I wrote, directed, and hosted a television series for public access in Los Angeles called "Act *BIG!*" It was a half-hour program that ran in thirty-one cities in the Los Angeles area for six months. The body of the show consisted of scenes and monologues performed by students in my acting classes. It gave my students a venue in which to perform and have their work seen all over Los Angeles. I called the show "Act *BIG!*" because I believed that this challenge to the actor: "Who do you think you are to be an actor and do something so enjoyable in the face of all this suffering?!" needed to be addressed. People try to put you down—and keep you down—for doing something that they wanted to do but didn't have the courage to do themselves. "Who do you think you are? You think you're really *big*, don't you?" they cry.

Who do we think we are? We are angels on assignment to lessen suffering by those very acts of creative self-expression that the blocked ones find threatening but that, in fact, entertain, educate, and enlighten—even *them*. The blocked ones think that you are altruistic and noble only to the degree that you are suffering. But those people don't understand that you can enlighten others only when you, yourself, shine.

Yes, we do think we are big! Because we know who we, and all others, are. Yes, do act *big*. You are big, so act big. What is the alternative? To act small? Which way honors our creator more? So claim your right to be an actor if that's what you want to do. As Roseann Barr said, "The thing [people] have got to learn is that nobody gives you power. You just take it."

SUMMARY OF MAIN POINTS

1. Acting is a calling.
2. Acting as a calling is as worthy of respect as any other calling or mission.
3. The universe governs by desire. You know that you are called to be an actor if you desire to be one.
4. Although our choice of occupations is limited, each option constitutes an effective spiritual workshop in which to develop and express our individuality, as well as an opportunity to contribute to the well-being of our society.
5. Honor and respect your own desires and the purity and altruism of your motives.
6. If you seem to have several, even conflicting, desires, choose the one or ones that to you seem the most *grand* because that's what you truly desire.
7. Gently but firmly does it. Your desire has within it all that it needs for its fulfillment. You don't have to push with your will. Just *want* it.
8. You do your best for others when you do what you truly want to do.
9. You do not need to save the world; the world is already saved. *Love* the world, and contribute to its ongoing well-being by being magnificent.
10. Act *big!* Be spectacular. Come into your own and be a role model for others. That is more pleasing to our cosmic parent than fear, complaining, and dissatisfaction. That's really doing something!

CHAPTER 23

Clarifying and Aligning Your Motives

Don't ask yourself, "How do I do this?" Ask, "Why am I doing it?" Then the character will decide your action.

—Robin Phillips, director

How does one bring to mind his primary purpose? As individual expressions of life, our primary purpose is the same as the primary purpose of life, itself. What is the purpose of life? The purpose and business of life itself is to be perfect magnificence, to radiate splendor—to be all that it can be, and to expand upon that forever. So then, we, too, as the individual representatives of life, have the purpose and privilege of expressing our capabilities and talents to the fullest. We, too, are to be absolutely magnificent. Which is not a bad gig, is it?

⊛ Affirmation

I am the glorious gift of life. I am thoroughly stylin'! I am pure, I am loved, and I am safe.

※ EXERCISE

Please complete the following sentences with whatever first pops into your head:

1. You know, ever since I was a small child I've always known that _____

2. You want to know why I really think we're here? OK, I really think we're here _____

3. I'm going to tell you a secret: _____

Now review what you've written. It's always great to take a look at what you really think, which, often, is more easily done when you've got it down on paper.

ONLY THE IDEAL IS THE REAL

One of my teachers suggested to me that whenever someone asked me how I was, I respond, "I couldn't be better, thanks." His point was that if I would cultivate the habit of claiming that spiritual fact as my answer, the proclamation would have the effect of lifting me to the height of the truth in it. In exchange for that, I would have to sacrifice the morbid pleasure that comes from complaining, but he made me see that even that valued treasure was really a small price to pay for conscious and dependable well-being!

We *are* well. We truly *couldn't* be better. And we achieve the execution of our purpose to be fabulous by aligning ourselves daily with what—when we don't yet feel it—only seems ideal. But only the ideal can be truly realized; everything else is illusion.

To Pontius Pilate, Jesus stated his life purpose. He said, "To this end was I born and for this cause came I into the world. . . ."

243

EXERCISE

OK, hold it. If you don't already know, what do you think he said that cause was? Take a guess, if you will. It will be interesting for you to check your guess against Jesus's answer. Try it. Guess, from the depth of your soul:

"To this end was I born and for this cause came I into the world ____
____
____
____."

Now, before I tell you what Jesus said, give yourself credit because there is truth in whatever you said because it came from what *you* think *your* right purpose is. Now let's see what Jesus said: "To this end was I born and for this cause came I into the world: *that I should bear witness unto the truth.*"

I'll bet your answer was somewhat similar. Now let me ask you something else. Does good acting in a good play do anything less? Does it not bear witness unto the truth about life?

IN DRAMA THE GOOD GUYS AND THE BAD GUYS ARE EQUAL

Whether you play a good guy or a bad guy in a play, you contribute equally to the unfolding and delivery of truth to an audience. You are contributing to the collective effort of revealing truth in either case. So play whichever type of role you think you can do best. The character Othello, for instance, was besieged by jealousy. Do we not, as an audience, gain tremendous insight into our own psyches and the way that jealousy can torment us when we see that play? Iago was a cruel instigator in the same play. Do not the actors who represent that state of mind contribute by illustrating the trouble that deceit can cause in people's lives? Of course they do. Those are just two examples—from the same play, no less—of the fact that it doesn't matter whether you play good or bad guys, so long as the truth is served.

EXERCISE

Please write a three-sentence prosperity prayer affirming your willingness to serve wherever your talents can best be utilized, as well as your undeniable right and access to abundant supply and well-being *now;* then pray your prayer with fervent sincerity until you are convinced of its omnipotent veracity.

____

____

____

____

____

____

THE ACTOR'S PURPOSE

The actor's aim, therefore, is to express his insight and talent to be a living witness to the magnificence that is life. That is your function *and* your desire, is it not? Trust it; follow it. Trust, too, that everyone else is being guided to do what he or she wants to do as well and that your goals will not conflict but intersect and link up with those of others for the good of all. Individually and collectively we will continue to evolve into a higher experience of how fantastically beautiful life is.

THE ACTOR'S MISSION STATEMENT

Often, the principals in a business organization will draft what is known as a mission statement. This statement encapsulates the primary purpose of the business, including its function in society. I believe that it is appropriate, and eye-opening, for each of us to put together a mission statement that captures the purpose of our individual work in the world. How would you state the mission of the actor? Give it a shot, and then I'll give you mine.

The mission of the actor is: _____

_____

_____

_____

_____

Here's mine: The mission of the actor is to fulfill his or her potential by expressing the truth that blesses others with healing insights. Or, in the words of the actor him- or herself: "My mission or purpose is to glorify truth by blessing others with healing insights," a purpose that is noble and worthy of respect.

We all want to know that our purpose is worthy of respect. We want that feeling of self-esteem that we get when we know we are doing our part in the family business—the business of the human family, the business of life. We can't, in fact, become relaxed, fearless, and free from anxiety until we know that we *are* doing our part in the family business, which then makes us feel worthy of success. For we feel worthy of success only when we know that we have our feet planted firmly on spiritual ground.

If your motives are straight, then, don't you agree that as an actor you are doing pretty good work here on the planet? So now let's get down and dirty. Let's debunk the sour-grapes accusations of actors that would try to keep us from achieving our bliss.

DEBUNKING THE SOUR-GRAPES ACCUSATIONS

✖ EXERCISE

Please list five negative things you have heard said about actors or acting:

1. _____
2. _____
3. _____
4. _____
5. _____

The main sour-grapes accusation or allegation says—and I'll bet it showed up somewhere in what you've written above—"actors have giant-size egos; actors are selfish and vain." We've all been told that, haven't we? We're made to feel guilty or selfish about acting because it's so much fun! It's fun, so it must be wrong! Pay now, play later, we are counseled. Fine, except there is no later. There is only now. Every instant of reality exists only in the now. We can think about the future and we can think about the past, but we only ever *experience* the present. So let's develop the habit of experiencing our bliss now, because *now* is the only time we are ever going to get a chance to do so.

Do what you want to do, now. This is one of the rewards you get for taking the time each day to clarify and align your motives—you reap a calm, confident clarity that things are in order and that you are safe and secure. You are able to see that you are *meant* to have fun in what you do, and that there is nothing wrong or sinful in that. *Sin* is an archery term meaning to "miss the mark." You miss the mark when you're *not* happy, not when you are, because the bull's eye is being happy.

✖ EXERCISE

Please list five things or activities that make you the happiest:

1. _____

2. _____

3. _____

4. _____

5. _____

Now, by signing below, please signify your agreement that you promise to experience at least three of the things you have listed above within the next week.

Agreed: _____

"Actors have big egos." Phooey! That is incorrect. Big balls, maybe. Because it does take a lot of courage to act. And it takes a lot of work to do it well. But not only do the people who wish *they* were doing it say actors have big egos, actors themselves say it about one another. As an actor, please watch this. If you accuse someone else, the allegation is going to have a negative effect on your own self-image as an actor, which will work against your achieving your own success. That makes sense, doesn't it? If you think Actor A is a creep for being an actor, then you're not going to go for it 100 percent unreservedly yourself, are you? Psychologically, subconsciously, you'll be holding yourself back. It's like the man who wants money but goes around saying that people with money are jerks or that money is dirty and that you should wash your hands after handling it. This guy is not exactly helping himself get more money, is he? It's a bit confusing to the subconscious. He's saying it's bad but he wants it. No. Money is good. Money is gorgeous. Money is "OK with me." It's money, honey! In fact, let's vamp in place right here for a moment.

✳ EXERCISE

Please write an eight-line poem about the attributes of money, to money itself:

ODE TO MONEY

_____

_____

_____

_____

_____

_____

_____

_____

Great. Now memorize and recite it to three different people you have heard criticize people who have money.

Yes, money is good. It is the idea of abundance made manifest. There's nothing wrong with it at all. And neither is there anything wrong with getting up there on stage and strutting your stuff by representing truth for an audience. On the contrary, there is everything right about that, too! It always hurts me when I hear actors putting other actors—or themselves—down. Don't buy that nonsense "actors are vain," or any other sour grapes accusation. They originate with people who don't have the courage to do what you are doing and want to keep _you_ from doing it, too! God bless them, feel sorry for them, even help them if you can; but don't let them rain on your parade. You don't have to put your life on hold simply because somebody else did.

ALIGNING WHAT YOU HAVE CLARIFIED

We can see, then, that to avoid a sense of neurosis, our vocation and our spiritual calling must be one and the same. Then the accuser is not there: The one who says you are selfish and vain for doing what, to you, seems wonderful and fun. On the contrary, I am good and obedient for doing what seems wonderful to me.

Now that your motives to be magnificent, to honor truth, and to help others are clear to you, you will begin to feel more comfortable and fearless in your work each day, because one follows the other. If we occasionally forget, thinking that we *are* working primarily for the by-products of wealth, power, fame, and pleasure, putting them before our deeper motives to be and to serve, we temporarily lose our light. We become anxious again, the pain of which quickly gets us right back on track. So, no big problem. In our heart of hearts, we all know that we should be—and we want to be—participating in the family business and that we're not going to get deep enough satisfaction from our careers until we are doing that.

ACTING IS NONDENOMINATIONAL

One of the things that is beautiful about dramatic acting is that it is nondenominational in its elucidation of truth. It deals with the human condition shared by all men and women—the priests, the rabbis, the blacks, the whites, the Republicans, the Democrats, the straights, the gays, the you, the me—all of us. It is also extremely tolerant. It deals with all issues with which people are confronted. None are excluded. The more on the fringe or controversial, in fact, the better theater it produces. If there is something one doesn't talk about, it will be talked about in theater. And sometimes *only* in theater. Often it's only the practitioners of the theatrical arts—the writers and directors and actors—who have the insight and the courage to talk about it. Theater is a wonderful, magnificent forum for the explication and elucidation of truth. And we, the practitioners and the audience, are the beneficiaries of her bounty.

THE IMPORTANCE OF EXPECTING SUCCESS

We are all beneficiaries of all that is good. We get to witness *and live* that which is good. We get to demonstrate it, express it, prove it, be it. And we get to enjoy it. Not because of anything that we did to earn that beneficent state of affairs, but because that is the way that life is. Life is good. And when we are confronted with the suggestion that it isn't, we have the power to demonstrate otherwise.

In our acting, therefore, let us remember that we are doing a grand work that has all the power of the universe behind it to help us succeed. Let our prayer be, "Thank you, God. Of course I am being successful. How natural it is. Success is inevitable because you and I are one and we are absolutely magnificent! What even greater glory can I expect next? In what next even greater achievement will I succeed? I am open to it and I accept it. Furthermore, I gratefully *expect* it."

❋ EXERCISE

Please write the truths, as they occur to you, that debunk the five sour-grapes accusations that you listed earlier.

1. ____________________
2. ____________________
3. ____________________
4. ____________________
5. ____________________

SUMMARY OF MAIN POINTS

1. The purpose of life overall is to be magnificent; the purpose of each of us individually is to be magnificent.
2. The actor's mission statement might be stated as: "My mission is to glorify truth by blessing others with healing insights." This purpose is as altruistic as any on Earth.
3. Unless our motives are pure, we will not feel worthy of success.
4. Actors have gotten a bad rap; they have been accused of being selfish and vain. But this is untrue. Deep in the heart of every actor is the desire to help his brother and sister.
5. Adopt the actor's golden code, to love one another and refuse to put one another down.
6. In proportion to your expectation of success does it manifest in your experience.

CHAPTER 24

Integrating the Actor's Purpose

An actor is someone who wants to be seen in order to share the discoveries he has made about himself.
—Dustin Hoffman

You are now clear about what your purpose is. You have given yourself permission to do it, have claimed your right to do it, and have seen that doing what you want to do is the only way to find your right niche and to make a contribution to the world. Now you need to make sure that all the facets of your career, as well as all the different parts of your life, are harmoniously integrated so that you are living as a whole. You need to be sure that you have no conflicting motives or aspirations, and that everything you do, think, feel, believe, want, and love works together as a seamless life, furthering your overall spiritual aims.

INTEGRATING ACTING AS AN ART, A CALLING, AND A BUSINESS

As an actor, your *calling* is to serve society by the *art* of elucidating for people truth as it may be applied in human affairs. But are you clear enough that you must also practice this altruistic art as a *business?*

The Purpose of Acting As an Art
The artist expresses himself—his vision and point of view. That is his motivating impulse. We all feel that impulse. And as we follow it, we fulfill and relieve ourselves while, at the same time, we benefit society by our contribution—in much the same way that a tree, when it exhales, relieves itself of its bounty that serves the animal kingdom in the form of fresh air. The purpose of acting as an art, then, is to express one's desire—one's *need*—to demonstrate and share one's insight and understanding of life.

The Purpose of Acting As a Calling
This aspect of your career, which is devoted to helping others and serving God, has been well covered, particularly in chapter 22.

The Purpose of Acting As a Business
But what is the purpose of acting as a business? The purpose of acting as a business is to make money. It is to gain, to increase, and the symbol of increase in our society is money. Money: My Own Never-Ending Yes-ability! The wherewithal to achieve our desires. Money doesn't get us all our desires—we know that—but it does get us a lot of them, like shelter, food, clothes, entertainment, transportation, and gifts. So we want it. Lots of it. Can't have too much money! In fact, we *have* to have it. And we have a right to have it.

The desire for money seems selfish to many who are artists or are on a spiritual path. Does it seem selfish to you? Remember, selfishness is a much-maligned state of mind. Selfishness is negative *only* if it denigrates the value of the other. Love your neighbor as yourself, but *not* better than yourself, or instead of yourself, or before yourself. Taking care of yourself takes nothing away from the other but, in fact, benefits him by inspiring him to do the same; for the universe governs by the brilliant efficiency of self-government.

You and I need to make a living. Those are the cards we're dealt here on the planet. We call that business. And we need to succeed in this effort. The business aspect of your career, then, is that aspect by which you collect your due for your service. That's why businesspeople often say, "I'm not in business for my health; I'm in business to make money." They are claiming their right, against many obstacles, to make money. "I'm not in business to make people happy," they say, to pep themselves up to get out there and bring home the bacon.

These statements are misleading, though, because you *are* in business for your health and to make other people happy. It's healthy for you to express yourself in your art, and it does make people happy when, as a result of your products and services, they are blessed. But in the business aspect of your acting career, you are doing it for what you can get; you are doing it for the money. And that is fine. You do not give your service for free. Say that, please: "I do not give it for free." You do it for balanced remuneration because you need to eat. And it is up to each individual to walk up to the table to claim his bounty: "I am in business to make money. I am in business to receive. I am in business to get, every bit as much as I am in business to give." Just make sure that your getting and giving are balanced.

The purpose in your art is to express yourself, the purpose in your calling is to help others, by which you also glorify the collective, and the purpose in your business is to receive the money and contacts and to develop further opportunities that keep you continually progressing. These three aspects of your acting career must be harmoniously integrated for you to be clear and at peace in your work.

KNOW THAT YOU ARE VALUED AND NEEDED

Be clear, please, that what you have to offer as an artist is needed not only by life as a whole, but by every individual expression of life. Know, as well, that your contribution is welcomed with open arms. Have faith in this sometimes less-than-apparent truth, and watch this faith prove to be "the substance of things hoped for."

In metaphysics it is not rare that a truth must be claimed, believed, and held to before it is perceived by the senses to exist. By the spiritual law of the coincidence of supply and demand, however, you can trust that what you have to offer is needed, desired, accepted, appreciated, and remunerated. The need for your product exists as soon as your product exists. The artist knows that his or her function of gathering grandeur from the heavens to lay at the feet of society is a sanctioned one, deserving of approbation and profit; it is society itself, in fact, that creates the artist to bring that vision to it.

❈ *Affirmation*

> *I know who I am, what my purpose is, and that life itself is seeing to it that I shall succeed. I am confident, peaceful, and grateful.*

INTEGRATING THOSE DASTARDLY DEPARTMENTS

Before you are able to successfully integrate acting as an art, a business, and a calling, you may need to do some pretty thorough and constructive mental housekeeping. To do that, you'll need to integrate what I call the "dastardly departments" of your life.

What are these dastardly departments? We have our private life, our family life, our social life, and, if we're lucky, our sex life. We have our sports or exercise life and our work life. We have our creative life, made up of things we'd really like to do the way we would really like to do them; our secret life, made up of things we know we shouldn't do but want to do anyway; and our spiritual life, constituted of things we know we really should do. We have all these seemingly separate little departments with their "have to do's," "should (or shouldn't) do's," and "would like to do's," and, unfortunately, they don't always agree.

These are the dastardly departments of our lives, and dastardly they are. This is when our whole psyche feels divided. This is that "divided kingdom" that's in danger of falling on its ass! One area of our consciousness is going in one direction, another is going in another, and another—who even knows? And we feel flipped out, unsettled, and unfocused—unable even to fathom what our work *is,* let alone get down to it. Let's take a look at these so-called departments.

OUR PRIVATE LIFE

Our private life comprises the things only we know about ourselves, the things we don't tell anyone else; the parts we want to keep to ourselves in our precious, psychic jewelry boxes. It's the part of us that knows that we don't need anything from anybody else because we are already complete beings. The part that knows that if we get a divorce, we are going to be all right; that if we lose our jobs, we're going to be OK; and that even if nobody likes us now, we're still going to be OK. Our private life is constructed of the things we do when we need to be by ourselves. We need that time, and we must take it. We must take time for contemplation and meditation and prayer, time to take care of ourselves, love ourselves, give ourselves warm baths, treat ourselves to our favorite candy bar, and go to a movie in the middle of the day. This is where we learn to know what we really want to do with our lives and give ourselves permission to do it.

OUR FAMILY LIFE

Our family life is our relationship to those closest to us—our parents, our siblings, our lovers, our children, and our closest friends. Are we taking time for these people, and are they taking time for us? Are we honest with them; can we expect them to be honest with us? Are we nurturing one another?

Yes, we are growing. We are finding adult ways to deal with our family intimates, to clear away the terrible neuroses that, like jagged barnacles, encrust our hearts, and by doing so, we open ourselves to love. We are becoming more willing to sort out the past and deal with the present. We've become more respectful of ourselves, and we have stopped accepting abuse. We more consciously love ourselves and one another, don't we? And we are learning that this family "department" of our lives must not conflict with our private life, because unless the way we behave with our family harmonizes with the way we think and feel in our innermost private moments, we will not be able to avoid unhappiness. To be happy, our beliefs, our actions, and our interactions must always harmonize with one another.

OUR SOCIAL LIFE

Our social life is made up of the experiences we share with our friends and acquaintances. The way we are and behave with our friends—although we behave somewhat differently with each person because we mirror different aspects of one another—should not be much different from how we are when we're with our families or by ourselves.

The goal in our life is integrity—freedom from psychic deceit and moral compromise in every condition and situation so that if someone were a fly on the wall and observed us, first by ourselves, then with our family, and then with our friends, he would see no phoniness or deceit, but a consistent, seamless fabric of integrity. We all want to live like that. We want that strong, fearless sense of ourselves that cannot be shaken by any effort of intimidation. We're not pretending we're one thing while really being another; we're *us,* all the time.

OUR SEX LIFE

We talk about our sex life and our love life interchangeably, don't we? How's your love life? How's your sex life? Well, it should be magnificent! It should be wonderful and exciting, filled with romance and delight and pleasure. And it should also be in balance with the rest of your life. Sex is like dessert. It's something we definately want in our lives, but we need to keep it in balance so it doesn't take too much of our attention away from the other areas of our life, which, as powerful as it is, it can easily do!

I believe our work is more valuable to us than our sexual and social relationships because I think our work is more deeply and critically tied in to who we are as individuals, as well as to our overall purpose on Earth. What we have to give and do on our pilgrimage here is, ultimately, more important to us than the pleasures of interrelating with lovers and friends we meet along the way. Our relationships, in fact, exist primarily to support us in our work. And if they don't, they have to go. After all, you wouldn't allow someone to *enter* your life who, at the outset, you knew would try to keep you from your work, would you? No. Your work is more important to your sense of who you are and your sense of satisfaction than any emotional (or physical) payoff you may mistakenly agree to exchange it for. And knowing that keeps you strong in your*self.* The people you meet along the way come and go, but your work is something that you take with you when you leave.

That said, you do need to have satisfying relationships. But they are to support you, your ambitions, and your mission. So please get with people who are supportive of you, and only stay with them as long as they are. You can't afford to waste your life with petty tyrants.

OUR SPORTS OR EXERCISE LIFE

Exercise is crucial. We need to work out or play some kind of sport. It helps to keep the cogs and gears running smoothly. It makes you feel good. It makes you feel agile and flexible and young. The type of exercise you choose should be in concert with your individual makeup, rhythms, values, and style. Is modern dance or ballet—expressing grace and control—more true to your nature than pumping iron? Or would pumping iron—expressing strength and intention—be more suitable? Do whatever works for you, whatever feels good and natural. Use desire as your guide. Whatever you want to do, whatever makes you the happiest—that's what you should do. If you will let desire guide you in all the disparate departments of your life, the departments will begin to play in concert with one another until they merge. Then the fabric of your life will manifest a certain satisfying seamlessness. All begun, perhaps, because you started playing weekend softball, because you wanted to!

OUR WORK LIFE

Our work life, our career life: we've been focusing on it throughout this book, specifically your career as an actor. But when looking at your career as an aspect or department of your overall experience, it is critical to see that—for you to be happy—it, too, must harmonize with all the other notes in this psychic symphony of your life.

I know a man who categorized his life into three departments: writing, family life, and martial arts. That was it. He did nothing else in life, nothing that did not fall into one of those three areas—at least, so he said. He got up in the morning and he either hung out with his wife and daughter, or he practiced martial arts, or he wrote. That was it. I'm not sure how things were with his family, but I know that he was a master in martial arts and a science-fiction writer with many bestsellers and awards to his credit. My acquaintance (certainly not my friend—he had no time for friends!) had honed his life, excluding everything except that which satisfied him most. His case was radical, and I'm not sure how long it all lasted. For all I know, he's now divorced, smokes pot, and refuses to write another damn word. But I do give him credit for the fact that, at least for a while, he focused and had discipline; he integrated the aspects of his life that meant the most to him into a whole. Are you doing the same? Is your work life expressive of who you truly are? If not, or not enough, you still have some work to do.

OUR CREATIVE LIFE

As an artist, your work life and your creative life are already one. They are already integrated. If you are not an artist, then you will need to forge that connection yourself by realizing that not only is your work—no matter what it is—actually quite creative, everything you do in your life can be creative. The way you fold your clothes and put them in piles can be creative. The way you arrange the items in your desk drawers can be creative. The way you design every meal can be creative. In fact, it *is* creative, however you do it; so why not allow it to be more consciously so? Life is more satisfying that way.

Your work in society is creative because it contributes to the creation and maintenance of a well-functioning society. We are creating the world we live in—look at how radically the computer industry has changed our world. Our every action has an impact. Even if you are doing the smallest, most mundane, and least important task in all society, your contribution—like the smallest part in an engine—is crucial to its overall performance. I believe that every one of us has the creative bent and that we all need some outlet for the expression of that creativity. Furthermore, I think that we will be happiest if we devote our lives to *being* that outlet so that everything that we do, we do creatively.

Let our every action be impeccably creative. Let the trunks of our automobiles, our closets, and our file cabinets be, not only not messy, but creatively arranged. Let every area of our lives be well functioning and pleasing to behold. Why not? Because we don't have the time? Because it takes too much effort? We *do* have the time, and it *doesn't* take too much effort. Again, let your desire be your guide. Your future is bright with promise. You get to do what you want and you get to do it with great creativity.

OUR SPIRITUAL LIFE

Notice I skipped our secret life. That's because if all the other departments of our lives are well integrated, we will no longer have a secret life. There will be nothing to hide anymore. We will have woven together one seamless spiritual life.

Our spiritual life can often seem the most dastardly department of all because we may think, "Gee, I really should just be holy—which I'm *not*—and not do anything else at all. Especially not anything fun!" In addition, religion often seems to encourage us to think that other's views on life—if they differ from ours—are wrong, which can make this department the most divisive of all.

It is not spiritual to think that we are supposed to plant ourselves on some mountaintop and vegetate (OK—*meditate*). Anybody could do that. *That* would be a piece of cake. It's living in the world that takes spiritual balls! Life is for living—on the field, in the market place, in the world. Buddha came to that realization. Meditation and prayer are simply part of that effort.

Your spiritual life is your overview. It's the mental pinnacle where you are able to see that life itself is integrated as one harmonious whole, that all the aspects of your life are one, and that all other beings are but different expressions of the same one being that you are. Spirituality opposes the suggestion that we are separate from our source, separate from one another, separated within ourselves, and separate from our income, our opportunity and our success. Spirituality is the truth that we are *one* with our joy and bounty.

Please remember how important it is to spend some time every day doing your spiritual work. It makes all the difference in the quality of your experience and better equips you to integrate all the areas of your life into a seamless whole. Know that you are in right relationship with every aspect of your *self!*

✖ EXERCISE

Please write down an ingredient that you consider necessary to the health of each of the following so-called departments of your life, which contributes also to the harmonious interaction of all of them.

Your Private Life: _____

Your Family Life: _____

Your Social Life: _____

Your Sex Life: _____

Your Sports Life: _____

Your Work Life: _____

Your Creative Life: _____

Your Spiritual Life: _____

SUMMARY OF MAIN POINTS

1. Now that you are clear about what your purpose is and have claimed your right to fulfill that purpose, you must be sure that the seemingly separate departments of your life are harmoniously integrated so that you live as a whole.

2. The purpose of acting as an art is to express yourself. The purpose of acting as a calling is to help others, by which you glorify the whole. The purpose of acting as a business is to gain and increase—to make money, contacts, and develop further opportunities that keep you progressing. Integrate the three-pronged purpose of acting as an art, a calling, *and a business!*

3. Trust that what you have to offer is needed, desired, accepted, appreciated and will be remunerated! You will prove this in your experience in proportion to your understanding and acceptance of it.

4. Spirituality is the viewpoint from which we see that each of our lives is a functioning expression of the one perfect whole.

CHAPTER 25

Acting Is a Service Job

This is the true joy in life: being used for the purpose recognized by yourself as a mighty one.
—George Bernard Shaw

Acting is a calling, yes, and an honorable profession, but it is also a down-to-earth service job. You put on your miner's hat, pick up your actor's tool kit of experience and imagination, and say, "I'm going in!" Then you go in and explore the dark corners of the psyche to discover and later live for us on stage the emotional journey of your character. It's a tough job, and you must be courageous to do it because along the way you will be drudging up all kinds of as yet unresolved and painful elements in your own psyche as your means to relating to your character.

This sometimes makes acting even something of "a dirty job," but somebody has to do it! It's a dirty job in that there is often a great deal of emotional pain involved in acting. But to be an actor, you have to be willing to feel and, thereby, deal with the emotional pain that is a part of the human condition. That pain comes up for you as you identify and imbibe the experiences and emotions you will be portraying and feeling on stage. This takes courage, strength, and stamina, as well as honesty and great compassion. It takes work.

THE UNIVERSALITY OF THE JOB

Acting is a blue-collar, white-collar, turned-around-collar, no-collar job. It crosses the psychosocial, economic boards of our experience. As an actor, you must be willing and able to play any human being who has ever lived, no matter what his or her economic, social, regional, moral, psychological, or religious conditions were. Because within the mind that we all share are all the elements that, in varying degrees, make up each personality, none of which is foreign to any of us. Granted, the "bad guys" exercise a little more of the schmolike elements (or fewer of the virtuous ones) than the "good guys," but bad guys and good guys both have both good and bad characteristics in each of them. Although some of us are ashamed to admit it, we can all relate, to some degree, to everything that any of us does. It's the actor's job to facilitate that process of relating.

Yes, acting is work; and to be done well, it must be done as a service. In the old days, the actor was a "fool," the court jester. This was no happenstance view of him. The actor *is* and must be willing to be seen as a fool; he is a willing fool for love—for love of the society that he serves by his shameless portrayal of it. You, the actor, are love's servant. Are you willing to feel, to do, to be whatever is necessary to elucidate truth for your audience?

✖ EXERCISE

> Think about something that made you angry and makes you angry still. If you never expressed your anger about it, now's the time to let it rip! Say what you wish you had said to the mental object of your anger, whether it's a person or an event.

Precede this exercise by telling yourself that you are doing this as an acting exercise and that it will have no ill effects on you. Once you have had your temper tantrum, finish by proclaiming that the exercise was harmless to you. (Note: I recommend that you do this exercise when you are in your own house by yourself.)

THE ACTOR'S TO-DO LIST

Acting—although the results often seem to signify otherwise—is not magic. It is a cohesive and accessible process. There is no formula to it because every actor uses his or her own method, but however practiced, the art of acting is neither magic nor in any way secret or closed to all but a chosen few. It does require intelligent management, and dignity, however.

One way to help you tackle this big job of working on a role is to break the job down into a list of tasks. Below is an actor's to-do list, a guide for you to follow so that by the time you get on stage you will be thoroughly prepared and, therefore, deserving of great success for doing such a fabulous job!

1. **Create your character.** In your armchair (in your research, or when working with your director or coach) discover, and create if necessary, the experiences, motives, objectives, feelings, needs, desires, thoughts, and impulses of your character who, later, on stage or in front of the camera, is going to say and do what the playwright has prescribed for him or her, substantiated by your discovery and creation. Work during your personal preparation and rehearsals until you thoroughly understand, relate to, and imbibe the motives and impulses of your character.

2. **Learn your lines.** Note, though, that this is not the actor's first task. The actor's primary job is to feel. You don't get the cookie in acting for knowing your lines;

you get the cookie for feeling the feelings. The lines or text are but the extension or verbal expression of your character's feelings. You must first determine and then feel those feelings, as well as think whatever unspoken thoughts you choose as appropriate to motivate your lines before you say them. Because that's how it is in life: first the feelings, then the thoughts, and then the words.

3. **Rehearse rigorously.** During your research in your armchair, in the library, on the streets, and in counsel with others, you construct your character's past. But it is only when you begin to rehearse with the other characters—the other psychic constructions built by your *playmates*—that your character begins to live. Before that, he or she exists in a theoretical vacuum. But when your character begins to relate and interact with the others in his or her world, your character begins to *live*. It is during rehearsal that you refine and mold your character's persona until you are satisfied that your character, who now breathes with the life you have given him or her, is formed to serve the ends of the play. Therefore, rehearse as much as possible. Never skimp on rehearsal! Even if that means you and the other actors have to get together on the side to rehearse for free, do so.

4. **Commit fully.** Commit to the point of view or state of mind that is your character. *Mean it.* Mean everything that you, as your character, feel and say and do. You must lend your character your own credibility so fully that the truth behind the artifice of the drama becomes true for you and, consequently, true for the audience. Because when you know that the truth behind the artifice justifies the artifice, you so willingly and thoroughly suspend your own disbelief that the audience gratefully offers up theirs. That's part of the fun of acting, when — even if only for a short time—you forget that it is an act.

5. **Then live all that.** Bring everything you've done together —the thorough creation of the character constructed from your own experience and imagination, your memorized lines with their spine and subtext, your rigorous rehearsing and full commitment—and live it on stage. When you have done that, you have become an actor.

✵ *Affirmation*

I am a hard worker, a dedicated worker, a good worker, and no one can do this job of acting better than I can.

STAR OR SAINT?

Again, you do this work as a service. Forget the star stuff. That's not what acting is. That's the flip side of "Oh my God, I hope I can make it!," and it is just as damaging. That's the kind of off-track thinking that makes you feel separate from others, separate from yourself, your good, and your success—not to mention separate from the character you are playing—all of which creates terror. "I am a star!" No. You are an actor.

You are special. But you're special because everybody is special. And you didn't create yourself, so as wonderful as you are, you don't get the credit for it. Besides, you're really just doing a job. And *we're* hiring *you*, which means, you're working for us. And though it adds up, none of us pays you much for that service. If I call a plumber, I'm going to pay him much more money than I pay you when I go see your movie. So give us a break on the star stuff and be willing to give us good service, because that is what is really going on. You are serving truth to help us. Looking at it that way will keep you straight and free from fear.

✖ EXERCISE

Please list ten jobs you would like to do.

1. _____   6. _____
2. _____   7. _____
3. _____   8. _____
4. _____   9. _____
5. _____   10. _____

Please find and watch ten films in which each one of these occupations is practiced by the lead character. Note what human qualities and characteristics are common to all the characters and which ones are unique. More important, realize that they are all at your disposal for creating your characters.

THE ACTOR'S APPRENTICESHIP

Acting has an apprenticeship different from many other occupations—like plumbing, for instance—in that you don't make any money in the beginning. That's one of the ways that you make the cut as an artist. By working for free at first, you demonstrate that your substance and your satisfaction come from a higher, deeper, and less obvious place. You earn your stripes by proving to yourself and others that you are able—sometimes by working three other jobs—to stay on the field and on the stage and are, therefore, to be taken seriously as a player. You do this without receiving any remuneration for your effort besides the personal and spiritual rewards that accompany all acts of courage and come from your knowing that you are practicing, and progressing in, an art that you love.

It's a challenge to the artist to work this way. You feel somewhat foolish calling yourself an actor, a writer, a director, or a painter when you're not making any money at it. The first thing people will ask you when you say you are an actor is, "What have I seen you in?" Or if you say you are a writer, they'll ask, "What books have you had published?" When you answer none, you feel like an idiot. But you *are* a writer *if you are writing*, and you *are* an actor *if you are acting*—whether you are making money at it or not. Another reason it is hard for us to admit that we are actors before we have the world's corroboration is that we really want it, and we're afraid that we won't get it. But our apprenticeship demands that we proceed on our own instinct, desire, and faith at first *without* any guarantee of success. To the degree that we do that, we forge our fidelity into a formidable, tangible talent that, upon its very coming into being, is automatically demanded.

THE TERM OF THE ACTOR'S APPRENTICESHIP

How long does the apprenticeship take? For some it takes twenty, thirty years; others become good professional actors right away. Still others take the path of the art only and never make any money at it.

A woman in legal affairs at the Screen Actors Guild told me that many actors have satisfying part-time careers in acting and supplement their acting income by doing other jobs. Most artists, in fact, do not make a full living from the practice of their art; and yet, many do.

Your journey is an individual one; your path is unique. By adhering to the spiritual principles of success, you will find your own way and proceed at your own pace. Some people focus on their spiritual work early in their lives and don't really get to building their careers until later. And some start their career work early on and don't really catch on to the spiritual nature of life until later. Everyone's path is different, and each one is as good as the next.

What to do? Follow your heart and follow your instincts. Trust yourself. Be willing to put in the time—wherever your desire leads you—that your particular apprenticeship requires. Allow your career to develop its own perfect custom form. Then *remain* willing to do whatever is required of you; don't say, "OK, God, I can take it from here," when you get the first sign of success. Remain at your post as the humble, willing servant of truth that you, as an actor, are. You will then be blessed with the feeling that Jesus so enjoyed when, rising from the baptismal waters, he heard his father's voice say, "This is my beloved son in whom I am well pleased."

✷ EXERCISE

Please write a three-sentence prosperity prayer in which you ask God to guide you to become willing to be best used for life's highest purpose.

_____

_____

_____

_____

SUMMARY OF MAIN POINTS

1. Acting is a calling, but it is also a down-to-earth service job.
2. It's a "dirty job" in that there is often emotional pain; but the actor in service to society is willing to feel and, thereby, deal with that pain.
3. Acting goes across the psychosocial economic boards of our experience.
4. The job of acting is not magic.
5. Forget the star stuff. That's not what acting is. It's the flip side of "Can I make it?" Yes, you are special, but you are special because everyone is special.
6. This humble service approach to acting busts stage fright.

7. Acting has an apprenticeship different from many other occupations in that actors don't make any money at it at first.

8. Honor your path. Be willing to put in however much time your apprenticeship, and later the work, requires. It is from that standpoint of humble dedication that you will be blessed with the realization that you have done a good job.

CHAPTER 26

When Acting Becomes Healing and the Theater, a Church

If you want to send a message, call Western Union!
—Jack Warner

Cynics have interpreted the above statement to mean, "entertain; don't teach. And certainly don't preach!" But don't kid yourself; art is communication, and a function of all communication is to share truth. And an elemental key to the satisfaction of all actors is to be party to and witness the enlightenment of the people in their audience. After all, benefiting his audience is one of the actor's main objectives.

I venture that Warner was talking about skill and finesse, the *art* of the art. He didn't mean don't have a message. He meant convey that message with a light and steady touch so that the audience members will have benefited and will not have had their intelligence insulted.

What play—stage or screen—exists that we call great, however, that has nothing to teach us? And when acting is done right—when it is *true* and skillfully executed—not only does it teach us, acting becomes healing and the theater becomes a church, mosque, or synagogue. The theatrical experience enlightens and alleviates suffering so effectively that the audience doesn't know what hit them! And each audience member leaves the theater with his or her own emerald of enlightenment every bit as valuable as anything he might pick up at church.

THE EMERALDS OF ENLIGHTENMENT

1. **Insight and understanding.** An audience member may gain insight into something that is going on in her own life, or greater understanding about something that someone she knows is going through.
2. **Consolation.** Sympathy or empathy expressed by the characters within the play for one another over something similar to what an audience member is experiencing can give that member a tangible feeling of comfort and consolation.
3. **Forgiveness.** Seeing that the characters in the play have made mistakes similar to those he or someone he knows has made relieves the audience member of condemnation, guilt, and shame, and helps him to forgive himself or another.
4. **Justification and validation.** Rather than being helped to forgive himself or another, an audience member may suddenly see that he was *right* in what he did by some particular action, even though others may have condemned or chastised or ostracized him, with the result that he may have condemned himself. Having watched someone else (in the drama) go through a similar experience, he may now feel exonerated and once again worthy of his self-esteem.

5. **Encouragement and inspiration.** As an audience member sits witnessing the action and interaction during a performance, she may be encouraged to pursue her latent desires, to stay on track against all apparent odds, or to leave an outgrown position or unhealthy relationship. She may become inspired with a new idea or the answer to a question that has been bouncing off the walls of her mind.

6. **Entertainment, fun, and "a good time."** These may not be components of every church service, it's true, but they should be, don't you think? Good singing and a good, attention-holding lesson or sermon should not only be enlightening, but delighting! After all, there is nothing so absolutely satisfying as an attack of the cosmic giggles—those moments when you really grasp how the universe fits together and how perfect it all is. Entertainment, fun, and a good time are always present in good drama, even sad drama. Something in it delights us and turns us on.

When these precious jewels of enlightenment are present in theater, we can't help but receive certain insights. What Warner was advocating was a skillful transmission of these insights and messages, rather than hitting the audience over the head with them. And I agree with him.

✳ EXERCISE

Please complete the following sentences with whatever comes off the top of your head.
1. If I bring more awareness to my life today

_____

_____

_____.

2. If I take more responsibility for my choices and actions today

_____

_____

_____.

THE SATISFIED ACTOR

Once his or her work is done, the actor reaps great satisfaction from knowing that he or she contributed to the overall cosmic dance of progress by playing his or her part in it with skill, effectiveness, and dignity. Let's take a look at these three ideas—skill, effectiveness, and dignity—and their part, collectively, in making the experience of acting satisfying.

1. **Skill.** Spencer Tracy said, "Acting is OK, but don't let anyone catch you doing it!" Skill in acting is exercised when the actor really, truly _understands, identifies with,_ and then _expresses_ naturally the emotions and truths that combine to make up his point of view, state of mind, or character.

2. **Effectiveness.** Stella Adler said, "The first and most important approach for the actor is to read the play and find out what the playwright wants to say to the world." This seems obvious when you read it, but often an actor fails to read the whole play she has a part in! An actor executes her role effectively when, understanding the truth she is acting, she successfully communicates with and transforms her audience.

3. **Dignity.** Shirley MacLaine said, "A script has heroes, heroines, and heavies. After a while you have to grow to the point where you allow yourself to fall in love with the heavies, because the heavies are the great teachers of the lessons that must be learned by the heroes and heroines." The actor's dignity is in proportion to his

understanding that his work is a divine commission charged with healing power. His work contributes not only to the lives of his immediate audience, but to the lives each member of his audience then touches. This is tremendously satisfying.

Affirmation

I know that "all things work together for good" and that every member of society will benefit from my acting.

A GOOD DAY'S WORK

As actors, then, we represent states of mind that are a mixture of good and bad, strength and weakness, virtue and fault, joy and sadness, hope and depression, success and failure. It is our job to display these states of mind as truly and nonjudgmentally as we possibly can, so that the men and women in our audiences—our brothers and sisters, our fellow travelers, and our employers—may experience a moment of awakening and say, "Yes, this is true. This is how it is. This is how I am," or he is, or she is. They see more clearly than they did when they entered the theater; they have grown in the light of this truth revealed through the partnership between the playwright, the actor, and the audience. They may now leave with their gem of enlightenment—awakened, delighted, and enhanced. And after they have gone and the seats are once again empty, the theater dark and quiet, makeup and costumes removed and put away, the actor can then leave the theater with the peaceful yet resounding satisfaction of knowing that he or she has done a good day's (or night's) work, and that the world is a better place for his having played his part.

SUMMARY OF MAIN POINTS

1. Art is communication, and a function of all communication is to share truth.
2. Conveying the message of truth requires a light and steady touch so that the audience will have benefited by it.
3. If the play is good and well performed, each audience member will leave the theater with a gem of enlightenment as valuable as that which he or she might pick up at a religious service. And the actor will have reaped the satisfaction of knowing that he or she contributed to the dance of progress by playing his or her part in it with skill, effectiveness, and dignity.

CHAPTER 27

Wrapping It Up as a "Present"

It is a great piece of good fortune when an actor can instantly grasp the play with his whole being. In such happy but rare circumstances it is better to forget all about laws and methods, and give himself up to the power of his creative nature.

—Constantine Stanislavski

A RECAP ON WHAT IT IS YOU ARE DOING

How important it is to remember that we live in a perfect universe. I'll drop something, it'll go boom or crash, and I'll think, damn! Then I'll remember what Buckminster Fuller once told me, "You can't catch the universe off guard," and I'll think hey, what am I so upset about? The universe just operated perfectly.

All really *is* well. The spiritual principles of the universe really do function—properly, always—to facilitate our progress and success. It may look sketchy at times—as André Gide said, "One does not discover new lands without consenting to lose sight of the shore for a very long time," but eventually we find ourselves standing on solid ground. So relax and enjoy the process. To the degree that we do relax and trust the inevitable success of the process, we will enjoy life more fully each moment.

To that end, it's helpful to remind ourselves during our daily spiritual work that our occupations are spiritual workshops for our individual spiritual growth. Knowing this gives us permission to follow our hearts' desires; it explains why following our hearts isn't selfish. We are obeying the impulses of our God that exist to guide us along our pathways of learning. In your case, your impulses have led you to become an actor. Good for you. You are doing holy work by being an actor, and you know it. You—and the rest of us—recognize the great value you are contributing to society through this work. Congratulations! And thank you.

A RECAP ON HOW TO DO IT

Take your pre-moments before you begin to rehearse or step onto the stage to become aware, alert, and blazing! This is entering the vestibule of preparation, through which you pass from your world into the world of your character.

Next, be thorough in your armchair/research work in your early days of preparation on a part. Break down the role and build your performance step by thorough step. Earn your success by putting in the time necessary to do a good job. Then actually *be* that state of mind on stage for your audience.

To facilitate the success of the acting process on stage, do what you can *off*stage to imbibe the characteristics and qualities of life's greatest characters: our avatars, prophets, and priestesses; our philosophers, artists, and scientists. Learn from them how to be the loving, compassionate everyday person that each of the greats were; this, in turn, will help groom you to become an actor who is able to play anyone.

Don't do any of this too quickly. Don't take shortcuts. By being thorough and diligent, you will discover who you are in the constellation of dramatic actors, what *your* niche in the play is, and which types of roles you are most easily and obviously suited to play. Find that. Be willing to do that work, and you will also find that you will *have* work, satisfying work, because you will be coming from your unique area of expertise, which is a crucial part of the overall cosmic puzzle.

A RECAP ON OVERCOMING THE OBSTACLES TO DOING IT

We come across many obstacles in this world. It's important to remind ourselves that those obstacles are our friends, not our enemies. They are the means by which we grow. Everyone has them, and we seem to have them all day long. They come in all shapes and sizes; we even have them as each other.

How do we meet and master the obstacles to becoming a successful actor? One way is to learn how the business of acting is structured. Don't think that because you are special or charmed you're going to show up in New York or Hollywood and single-handedly restructure the business to suit your notions of how it should run. See how the system runs, and then find your way within that. You must first know the rules before you break them, if break them you must. When you remember that the true system is a spiritual system with *spiritual* rules, I believe you will see that, actually, they accommodate you nicely.

Remind yourself, too, that your opportunities arise from within your own consciousness. Although they come *through* other people, they do not come *from* other people. And they are as abundant as you need them to be for you to bloom. Be strict in refusing to accept the scarcity statistics that slap you in the face while you're trying to hold onto the goodness of life. Don't accept those fear-engendering miscalled facts that parade under the banner of "the way things really are in the real world." Use your spiritual authority to nullify these negative claims against the chances of your success. It's just fear, and fear is impotent.

Trust that God is good, in spite of all evidence to the contrary; *that's* the cut—maintaining trust *in the face of the seeming problem.* We all know how hard it is to take the bull by its horns and *make* things happen. So don't try so hard. Take the footsteps you're inspired to take, then fold your hands and smile. It is life's function to make sure that we prosper; it is our function to show up, do our best, and trust the process.

Remember, this is *your* life. You are not an extra in somebody else's movie; you are the star in your own life. Realize that you are endorsed by no less than the entire universe. Then get out there, find representation, and audition. *Now!*

A RECAP ON WHY YOU DO IT

Your business and other activities can overwhelm you unless you take time at the beginning and the end of each day to remind yourself that you really are on a spiritual pilgrimage here on Earth. So take the time. Remember that you have a mission and remind yourself what that mission is. Clarify and align your motives. Remember that your purpose is to shine, so that by your brilliance you contribute to the glory of life; acting is the service you offer by which you do that.

We have a strong work ethic, don't we? It's a part of human nature. We *want* to work, want to contribute, want to know that we have done something meaningful. Actors are no different from anyone else in this. What sets the actor apart is that, when we as actors have done our work well, our simple service transcends itself in the lives of our brothers and sisters by giving them greater light and understanding than they had before they came to see us work. When this happens, you, the actor, have done your job. It is *then* that you are a star.

THE PRESENT

We are entitled to success. I didn't say deserving of it because of our efforts, even though our efforts are part of the process and help us feel worthy of it. We are entitled to it because it just happens to be our good fortune that we are the expressions and recipients of all that is good.

So let's enjoy and live that reality. Whatever your particular path of creative self-expression is, don't put it off another day. Begin it today. Begin that wonderful process of self-expression that will make you fulfilled and happy, *now*. Get your photographs now. Start looking for an agent now. Audition now. Now is the only time, so the time to act is now. But remember, too, that you are becoming involved in a life-long process and need never feel pressure to get it all done in a moment. Learn to get in the groove, to "rest in action," and enjoy the process.

Another thing, dear one; don't worry. You are ready to take your next step. Fear can't stop you; you are the master in your experience. You have all the courage and talent of the ages residing within every cell of your being. You are absolutely magnificent, the best there has ever been. You have unlimited bounty to offer us. *You* are a present from God to us, an unfathomably wonderful gift. We thank God that you are in our experience, and we can't wait to see what you're going to come up with next!